D1291202   namic

The Six-Hat Salesperson

A Dynamic Approach to Producing Top Results in Every Selling Situation

DAVE KAHLE

AMACOM
American Management Association
New York • Atlanta • Boston • Chicago • Kansas City • San Francisco • Washington, D.C.
Brussels • Mexico City • Tokyo • Toronto

This publication is designed to provide accurate and authoritative information in regard to the subject matter covered. It is sold with the understanding that the publisher is not engaged in rendering legal, accounting, or other professional service. If legal advice or other expert assistance is required, the services of a competent professional person should be sought.

Library of Congress Cataloging-in-Publication Data
    The six-hat salesperson : a dynamic approach to producing top results in every selling situation / Dave Kahle.
        p.   cm.
    Includes index.
    ISBN 0-8144-0465-0
    1. Selling.   I. Title.
    HF5438.25.K34   1999
    658.85—dc21   99-20338
                                                                    CIP

Printing number
10 9 8 7 6 5 4 3 2 1

CONTENTS

PREFACE

I love sales. No, I'm not crazy; I'm blessed. The world of sales has provided me a career with a lifetime of challenge; unlimited opportunity to express my individuality, to make a good living, to grow as a human being, to create relationships and friendships, and to exercise all my gifts and talents. Very few people are blessed with all that.

I suppose it was my father who planted the seed of interest in me. He was a salesperson for a number of years and later became a branch manager. So when I was a teenager and was offered a job in retail sales, it was easy for me to say yes. Sales ran in the family.

The experience of selling men's clothing in an expensive retail store was my initiation into sales. I learned I had a knack for sales and I became the leading salesperson in the store. Later I took another baby step forward when, during the summers in my college years, I went to work for a company that sold housewares and groceries to households on a route. In that sales environment I was outside seeing people, instead of waiting for them to come into a store. Again, I met with some success and won a scholarship as the outstanding summer employee in a three-district area.

With that success under my belt, and after a few years of teaching, I was ready for my first full-time sales position, selling capital equipment to school systems. Eighteen months later I was the company's number one salesperson in the country and ready for a new challenge, selling surgical staplers to doctors in operating rooms. After a dismal start at that, I made more money than I thought possible and eventually left the company to go into business for myself, selling motivational and training products. Two years later, I sold that business and went to work for a sales recruiter, selling people's skills to sales managers. That led to my final full-time sales position, selling hospital supplies, and again I became the company's number one salesperson in the country.

In 1988, I began my current career as a professional speaker, sales trainer, and sales consultant. Since then, through my seminars and consulting projects, I've interacted with literally thousands of salespeople and their managers.

Through that checkered variety of sales experiences, I acquired the sales wisdom that I hope to pass on to you in this book. My intention is to make it easy for you to understand and implement that wisdom. As a sales trainer, I know that the biggest obstacle to sales performance isn't knowing what to do, it's doing it! So, from the very beginning, this book is designed to provide a system that you can put into practice. Every chapter has been designed to make it easy for you to implement the principals that are presented.

Four major components in the book support the objective of providing you with an easy-to-implement system. The first component is *principles*. Principles are bedrock, fundamental observations of deep truths. They express ageless concepts about human nature. Regardless of the ebb and flow at the surface of your life, principles remain unchanged. You can count on them always to apply. If you can uncover the key truths or principles that relate to selling, you'll have a foundation on which you can build for the rest of your sales career.

That the understanding of key principles is an important step toward success and maturity can be substantiated by reviewing a wide variety of sources. Look at Steven Covey's great concept of "principle-centered leadership" or review the work of an even more widely read author: Peruse the Bible and you'll discover the unveiling of principle after principle of human interaction.

While understanding principles is an important step, it's almost as important that you build on the *right* principles. For example, you may argue for the existence of a sales principle that states, "People are easily duped." While that principle may be true, it is *not* one on which you want to build a sales career. In this book, I've attempted to share my observations on the most important principles that affect sales success. Learn them and you'll be equipped with a wisdom that will serve you well for the rest of your life.

The second component is *processes*. Processes are the links that connect your understanding of principles to your behavior. Processes unleash the power of your potential by providing the how-to steps that help you actually implement the principles. They are often lacking in sales books, seminars, and training programs. Early in my career as a sales trainer and speaker, one of my seminar participants told me, "We've heard other people and they all have good things to say; but they never teach the *how-to* of implementing them. It's always, 'You should do this or you should do that,' but never how-to. That's what I like about your program. You show us the how-to."

The emphasis on how-to has been a hallmark of my work. I don't consider myself a motivational speaker, but I believe that my presentations are very motivational. I don't focus on emotional issues like many motivational speakers. Rather, I show people how to do something. My experience has taught me that knowing not just what to do, but how to do it is tremendously motivating. So the major thrust of this book is the how-to—the processes.

The third component designed to make the material easy to grasp is the use of simple *graphic images*. People often think in images. I learned a long time ago that if I could connect a concept to a simple graphic image, my seminar participants would remember it for years and find it easier to implement. You'll find graphic images throughout the book to illustrate almost every key concept.

The fourth component is the *anecdotes* from my sales experience that you'll find liberally sprinkled throughout the book. People relate to stories, and in my thirty years of selling I've accumulated a number of them.

The combination of principles, processes, graphic images, and personal examples is designed to help you make significant, powerful changes in your sales career.

If you are currently a professional salesperson, this book is designed to help you deal with the biggest issue of your career: responding effectively to the changes that are being driven by our culture's transformation to the Information Age. I'm thoroughly convinced that the skills and tactics that may have served you well in the past are being rendered obsolete. I can't count the number of salespeople with whom I have spoken in hundreds of sales training sessions who express pain and confusion over the changes they are being asked to make. This book is for you, to help you make the changes you need to make to become successful, ever-growing individuals in the new economy.

If you are a new salesperson you may be looking for shortcuts to success, ways to shorten the inevitable trial-and-error learning curve. This book is for you, to help you develop the wisdom necessary to become lastingly successful and enjoy the privilege I have enjoyed—a lifetime of challenge and opportunity.

If you are someone who manages salespeople, you may be looking for insights into the skills and processes to instill in your sales force. This book is for you, to provide you with a simple and powerful system to teach your sales force that will help them reach their goals.

Regardless of your position, it's my hope that your life will be just a bit richer and fuller as a result of the changes this book prompts you to make. This book is for you.

DAVE KAHLE

SELLING IN THE
INFORMATION AGE

What in the World Is Going On?

The Information Age is here, and it has brought with it transformational changes in the way successful salespeople must go about their jobs.

If you're an experienced salesperson, you're going to need to make some significant changes in the way you do your job. If you're just beginning your sales career, you need to understand what it's going to take to be successful. If you're a sales manager, you need to know what behaviors to encourage in your team. Regardless of your position, this book will open the door to success in the Information Age for you. The Six Hats hold the answers for each of you.

From my vantage point as a consultant and trainer to a wide variety of industries around the world, I have seen certain trends moving through our worldwide economy that are causing havoc among businesspeople in general and among salespeople in particular.

The changes coursing through economies around the world are revolutionary, like nothing we have ever seen before. Professional salespeople are caught in the middle of these changes. The strategies, skills, and concepts that used to work for you are no longer sufficient to ensure your success. They may be necessary, but they're not sufficient. The world is just too different now.

The new realities of the Information Age require a new paradigm for sales success, as well as a new set of principles, processes, and tools. That is what *The Six-Hat Salesperson* is all about.

Let's look at some of the characteristics of the Information Age.

Characteristics of the Information Age

Before we can discuss the particular pressures on salespeople, we need to examine the forces that characterize the Information Age and affect businesspeople around the world.

Imagine that each of these forces is an ocean current. An ocean current is an incredibly powerful, unseen force—maybe the most powerful force on the planet. Yet ocean currents are hard to see. We know where they are by observing the effect they have on things around them. We can see the flotsam and jetsam swept along in their paths.

So it is with the trends and pressures on businesspeople in the Information Age. They are like ocean currents: powerful, unseen forces coursing through economies and societies around the world, sweeping along everyone in their path—our customers, our competitors, our companies, and even our families.

When two or more ocean currents slam together, they create a treacherous, turbulent stretch of white water. The same is true of the trends moving through our economies. Like ocean currents, these trends merge and converge to form a whirlpool of turbulence.

Turbulence may be the most accurate adjective for the world today, the defining characteristic of the Information Age. As professional salespeople, you may sometimes feel as if you're hanging onto a piece of driftwood in the middle of permanent white water. Examining each of the currents involved will help you gain perspective.

THE FIRST CURRENT: RAPID, DISCONTINUOUS CHANGE

You've probably noticed that we're in an era of warp-speed change. Markets emerge, mature, and disappear almost overnight. New competitors appear out of nowhere. Hot new products become obsolete dinosaurs in months. Technologies change in the blink of an eye. Customers change rapidly. Our companies downsize, reengineer, and transform themselves. Welcome to the Information Age.

Perhaps Information Age is a misnomer. Maybe we should call it the Era of Change. It seems that everywhere we look, the world is changing faster than the images on an MTV music video. Certainly business environments around the world are changing more rapidly than at any time in our history. The problem is that this change is not a single event; it's a continuous process, and the pace or rate of that process of change is always increasing.

We've always had to deal with change. In fact, change may be a definition for life itself. If you're not changing, you're probably dead! I recall, in my days as a field sales rep, being very frustrated with one account. The account had a prime vendor relationship with my archcompetitor and, no matter what I did, I couldn't increase my meager business there. I ended up venting my frustrations to my manager, who counseled me to "Hang in there."

"The only thing you can be sure of," he said, "is that things will change. You need to position yourself to take advantage of those changes when they happen." Events proved him right. My competitor changed salespeople and experienced some service problems, and I had the opening I had been waiting for.

So, we've always had to deal with change. It's the rate of that change that is different now. Things are changing more rapidly than ever before. The force driving the rate of change is the explosion in the amount of information we're creating. That's why the era we live in is called the Information Age. Consider this: In 1900, the total amount of knowledge available to humans was doubling about every 500 years. Today, it doubles about every two years. That incredibly rapid pace of new knowledge production puts energy into the forces of change at an unprecedented rate. Some futurists predict that the total amount of information we have today will amount to less than 5 percent of what will be available to us in the year 2010.

It's not knowledge itself that causes change, but the application of knowledge. We see the application of knowledge in new products, new technologies, new customers, and new needs—all coming at an increasingly rapid rate. Like it or not, the conclusions, paradigms, and core beliefs upon which we based our decisions two years ago are likely to be obsolete today. Chuck's story is a good example of this.

Not long ago, my friend Chuck announced that he had to get out of the business he owned and find another one.

I was stunned. My first thought was, "Why on earth would he need to find a different business?" Chuck was living the American dream. Ten years ago he was a computer repairman who risked everything by leaving his job to develop his own computer repair business. In those ten years, Chuck had built an efficient, productive business employing fifteen people in two locations. His business had become stable and profitable; he was highly regarded by his clients; he had a good, loyal group of employees; and he was enjoying an income probably greater than he ever imagined. He was relishing the kind of situation most people only dream about. So why did he need to find a new business?

Here's what he told me. "In five years, I'll be out of business. Manufacturers are continually building computers that are smaller, cheaper, and more reliable. It won't be long before you won't repair them—you'll throw them away like you do a toaster. There won't be a need for the service my business provides."

Chuck's business was a winner in an industry—microcomputer repair—that will have come and gone in a period of about fifteen years. No matter how effective and productive Chuck is as a businessman, the rapid changes in our economy mean that the long-term prospect for his business is dim. Chuck was astute enough to recognize that before it was too late.

Two years ago the future looked great for his business. Today, it looks dim. Things have changed, and some of those changes that came about as a result of increased knowledge on the part of computer manufacturers. Think about it: An IBM PC was a revolutionary product and sold for about $4,500 when it was introduced a few years ago. Today, it probably doesn't even have scrap value.

Things changed. The application of increased knowledge resulted in new products that made that product obsolete. If that was true for the IBM PC and the host of products and variations that followed, think about what might happen to today's hot product. Regardless of how well researched, engineered, and manufactured it may be, it could become obsolete and worthless in two years!

One futurist has predicted that, by the year 2020, knowledge will increase at an astounding rate, doubling every thirty-five days! What that means for salespeople is that the rapid changes affecting almost every aspect of your business—products, markets, customers, etc.—will only continue to increase in speed. We live in a world that is changing more rapidly than anything humans have ever experienced before. This rapid change, fueled by increasing amounts of information, will continue to be the primary characteristic of the Information Age.

But there's another element to the current of rapid change. Not only is change rapid, but it's unlike anything we've seen before.

In his book, *The Age of Unreason,* Charles Handy makes a convincing argument that change today is "discontinuous." In other words, it doesn't necessarily evolve out of patterns or trends that we can predict. For example, the three major television networks coexisted quite comfortably for years. They competed with one another and gradually changed as technology and the tastes of their audience evolved.

Then, in a matter of a few years, cable television burst onto the field and the networks suddenly had hundreds of small stations and networks to battle. Their world was turned upside down by a technological development that changed things in a "discontinuous" fashion.

Rapid, discontinuous change: It's the first current surging through the Information Age.

THE SECOND CURRENT: RELENTLESSLY GROWING COMPLEXITY

Everywhere we look, every aspect of our business lives is becoming more and more complex. The explosion in knowledge means that the products we buy and sell are becoming increasingly complex. Automobiles are a good example. Last spring one of our family cars stopped running. It didn't gradually slow down or signal it's impending demise by running roughly. It just stopped, suddenly and without advance warning. It was as if the car announced one day, "I will run no more," and then shut itself down.

No matter what I did, I couldn't get it to start. A look under the hood revealed a complex array of wires and tiny black boxes that were totally new to me. Automobiles had become so complex that I had no idea what those little electronic boxes did, nor how to fix them.

Just a few years ago that maze of wires and electronics would not have been there, and the car wouldn't have been nearly so intimidating. I could have wiggled a wire, adjusted a carburetor, or done something to revive it.

The explosion of knowledge and the resulting complexity in my car left me intimidated and totally confused by what I saw under the hood. I gave up in frustration and had the car towed to the dealer. What did the dealer's personnel do to it? The mechanic hooked it up to a computer to find out what was wrong. The car had become so complex that even the mechanic—a victim of rapid change and growing complexity—couldn't diagnose the problem without the assistance of a computer.

Complexity seeps into every area of business, making it more sophisticated and intricate than a few years ago and ensuring that it will be even more so a few years from now.

If you work for a manufacturer, for example, chances are that your product lines are broader and more intricate than they were a few years ago. It's probably also true that many of the individual products you sell are themselves more sophisticated and complex than they were a few years ago. If you're with a service company, chances are that the services you sell are more complex and sophisticated than they were a few years ago. On and on it goes. On the product or service side of your business, it's likely that you are having to deal with considerably more complexity than ever before.

Product complexity is only one part of the relentlessly growing complexity current. Government regulation continues to grow, bringing with it layers of complexity that reach out and affect every area of our business lives. Think of the great tax reform act of 1990, or the Americans with Disabilities Act that ushered in an entirely new area of regulation. The number of regulations that businesspeople are expected to follow only continues to grow.

One last source of complexity is our friends, the attorneys. It seems that with every new law school graduate, the chances of getting sued for something increase. With every lawsuit we read about or hear about, we, of necessity, become more defensive in our practices. Thus the number of de facto regulations grows exponentially. With the U.S. claiming 70 percent of the world's lawyers, the prospect is great for this current to continue to swell.

Look at the tools and processes you use to do your jobs. I'd feel very comfortable in betting that they are far more complex today than they were a few years ago. I suspect that the computers you use, for example, are so complex that you're only using a tiny portion of their potential power. Before you begin to master the current models, new updates will appear that keep mastery too far ahead of you to be realistically achievable.

Finally, let's consider the expectations of your customers. I suspect that in recent years your customers have come to expect things of you that they didn't even imagine existed a few years ago.

Everywhere you look, every aspect of your job is growing more complex. This relentlessly growing complexity is the second characteristic of the Information Age.

THE THIRD CURRENT: CONSTANTLY GROWING COMPETITION AND CHOICES

As a vendor, do you have more competition today than you did three years ago? As a consumer, do you have more choices today than you did a few years ago?

Those two questions represent both sides of another current. As the rate of information expands, we're faced with more and more competition. That competition may or may not be coming from traditional sources, but it is certainly surfacing as growing choices for your customers. The issue of growing competition, or choices, seeps into every area of our lives, affecting us in almost everything we do.

Last summer my wife went to Florida for three weeks to help care for her ailing father, leaving me home with three of the kids. That meant I had to do the grocery shopping. It had been a number of years since I entered a grocery store in search of the family's weekly provisions. I had, of course, run in from time to time to pick up the miscellaneous one or two items that we needed for a special meal or that we had run out of in the middle of a recipe. But I hadn't had the responsibility for purchasing the family's regular supply of groceries. It had been fifteen years since I confronted a grocery store.

Do you realize what has happened in the grocery store in the last fifteen years? There, under one roof, is the quintessential example of all the currents we're discussing. If you had taken a photograph of a grocery store from fifteen years ago and compared it to one taken today, you would not recognize the two as being the same facility.

I muddled through the maze of options until I came to the cereal aisle. There, I stopped dead in my tracks. It was a revelation. Literally stacked from the floor to above my head, running the length of the entire aisle, were hundreds of choices in cereals. I was confused and overwhelmed. I didn't have time to read all the box labels, and every package was designed to pull my attention to it. In frustration, I resorted to ... Shredded Wheat!

My very real frustration with all the choices was a simple illustration of the third current surging relentlessly through our society—constantly growing competition and choices. The overwhelming number of choices I faced in that grocery aisle wasn't an isolated instance. In almost every area we look, under every nook and cranny of our economy, we are faced with an explosion of choices.

It wasn't so long ago that we had a choice of a handful of TV stations, for example. Today we can choose from at least forty. We're currently shopping for a new automobile for my wife. The choices are endless. Do we really need all these brands of cars? I could go on and on with examples, but they are evident everywhere you look. Just look at the options on the Web, which didn't even exist a couple of years ago. One of my clients remarked to me, and I agree, "There's just too much of everything."

There are two sides to this current. On one hand, it represents increased choices and freedom for consumers. On the other, it brings increased competition for vendors. Cereal and TV stations may be highly visible and universally recognized, but this trend affects almost every businessperson.

Competition is increasing for several reasons. There is, first of all, the explosion in alternate sources. For many traditional salespeople, discount warehouses, mail order catalogs, and telemarketing operations offer new choices to your customers, other ways to acquire the same products you sell. The technology revolution means that more and more processes are being computerized and the local computer consultant may be offering alternate ways for your customers to handle many of their processes.

As companies around the world downsize in response to increased competition, that trend creates even more competition. Many of the hundreds of thousands of laid-off white-collar workers will not find gainful employment in the industries they left. One survival strategy for many of them will be to start their own businesses.

Another source of increasing competition is overseas competitors. As the world becomes smaller due to improved transportation and communication technologies, foreign competitors are entering our markets. I have yet to work with an industry that didn't have a relatively new foreign player involved, and that's true worldwide.

Finally, our rapidly growing knowledge means innovations in technology. New technology means new choices for consumers and new sources of competition for vendors.

Ask yourself these simple questions: Do you have more competition today than you had a few years ago? Do you expect to see more competition in the future? The combination of rapidly expanding competition and options is another characteristic of the Information Age.

THE FOURTH CURRENT: CONSTRAINTS ON TIME

Friends called recently with an invitation for my wife and I to spend an evening with them. As we compared calendars, my wife and I discovered that it would be three weeks before we both had the same evening free!

Unfortunately, that was no isolated event. Our lives have become so full and so scheduled that we have very little "free time." I believe we're very typical. Franklin planners, Daytimers, and electronic calendars have become ubiquitous in business circles, a symptom of the growing number of commitments we make. When was the last time you made an appointment with someone who didn't have to wade through pages of commitments in an elaborately detailed calendar or consult an electronic version of the same? As we've become more aware of time and more committed to using it wisely, we also use it more fully, and leisure time is rapidly becoming a shrinking, precious commodity.

Unfortunately, work time is increasing at the expense of family and leisure time. Our guilt is rising in direct proportion—we're all trying to cram more productivity into the time we have. The extra leisure hours and minutes we once used to think about a strategy or situation have disappeared. We're in the quick-solution, rapid-fix mode, all due to the increasing pressure on our time.

Regardless of what is happening to other people, the really important question is, "Is this happening to you?" Ask yourself, "Do I have more pressure on my time today than I did a few years ago?" And, "Do I realistically expect to get more time or less time in the near future?"

If your answer to the last question is "less time," then you can personally relate to this fourth current swirling through the world of the Information Age salesperson, constraints on our time.

These four currents are surging through our society creating whirlpools of confusion and uncertainty—an incredibly turbulent time. Salespeople, like you, are being overwhelmed by these forces.

Implications for Salespeople

Every day, professional salespeople face new challenges and obstacles brought on by the rapid change that characterizes our entry into the Information Age.

Professional salespeople caught in the middle of this turbulence feel like they're being spun around in a whirlpool of confusion and uncertainty. The strategies and skills that have served them well in the past are no longer sufficient.

Over the last few years, in almost every sales training series or seminar I have presented, I've asked the participating salespeople to think about these trends and then to brainstorm what they see as implications of these trends for them. Professional salespeople have routinely identified a consistent set of challenges. Here's the consolidated list:

- **Time management.** Salespeople must become more effective in the use of their time. With the constant pressure on margins brought on by increasing competition, there's less and less room for slop. Salespeople must become adept at using their time in the most effective and efficient ways possible.

- **Productivity.** Salespeople must become more productive than ever before. It is not enough just to sell; you must now sell efficiently and effectively. The ubiquitous competition in every industry means that pressures on prices and profits will continue to grow. It is inevitable that companies will strive to find efficiencies that allow them to operate profitably with lower prices. Salespeople are no longer immune from the search for productivity.

- **Focus on the customer.** As the perceived differences between products melt away in the minds of the customer, it will be more and more important for the salesperson to understand the customer's needs, wants, interests, problems, objectives, and motivations. Instead of focusing on the product, successful Information Age salespeople will focus on the customer.

- **More training and education.** Products will come and go, programs will last for awhile and grow obsolete, and services will be eclipsed by the evolving needs of the customer. The salesperson equipped with today's knowledge—whether it be products, processes, or programs—will be equipped to deal with a world that no longer exists. The Information Age salesperson will need to constantly learn and grow, gaining competency with an ever-changing set of products, services, and programs.

- **More technologically astute.** Clearly technology now provides a means of increasing productivity for the outside salesperson. Like technology in every other field, it will continue to evolve. The salesperson will need to easily absorb the latest and greatest improvements in hardware and software, or risk being eclipsed by the competition.

All these implications reflect pressures on you, the salesperson, from the internal sources—your products and your company. There is, though, another set of pressures that have similarly sobering implications—the pressures on your customers.

Implications Resulting from Pressures on Your Customers

The sobering truth is that your customers live in the same world you do. They labor to stay afloat in the turbulent environment just as you do. Their worlds are more pressured, their time more precious, their lives more complex, their markets more competitive—just like yours.

The fact that your customers live in the same world you live in brings with it another whole set of implications for the Information Age salesperson. Let's look at each of the four currents from that perspective and consider the indirect implications on professional salespeople.

- **Rapid, discontinuous change.** This current means that your customers are quite likely to change some of the salient dynamics of their businesses. They could drop product lines, open new market segments, restructure, and transform just like your company. Your customers will be moving targets.

  You'll have to master good information just to stay current. Not only that, but the individuals on whom you call are liable to transform and migrate faster than ever. The days of calling on the same person for ten years are rapidly drawing to a close. Information Age salespeople will have to master the skills of building relationships quickly with a wide range of ever-changing individuals.

- **Relentlessly growing competition and options.** This current means that your customers probably have more competition in their businesses than they ever did, and that their businesses are more in jeopardy then ever before. You will have to be sensitive to the ebb and flow of their top lines.

  But your customers will have more options then ever before also, which means that you will need to be more sensitive to their preferences and intricacies so that you'll be able to position your product or service favorably in the light of the other ways your customers could satisfy their needs. Instead of focusing on your product or service, you'll have to focus on the customer.

- **Complexity.** Your customers' jobs are becoming more difficult and your customers are becoming overwhelmed with all the information they need to make good decisions. If you are going to win a respected place in their choices, you'll need to be a source of good, useful information to help them deal with the growing complexities of their jobs. You'll need to become their Shredded Wheat.

- **Constraints on time.** Constraints on time affect your customers in a number of ways. First, the days of stopping in without an appointment are over. People's days are just too structured and full to allow that. Second, your customers will have less time to make decisions about the products and services you sell, so you'll need to be more effective in your selling, compressing the time spent in the sales cycle.

So, we're in the Information Age. To a professional salesperson, that means the pressures of change, complexity, competition, and constraints on time will affect you not only directly but also indirectly, through your customers.

This is a time ripe with intense danger and rich in opportunity. The danger is that these pressures will make your job much more difficult. You may have to radically transform yourself to become effective. The skills necessary to be successful in the turbulent environment of the Information Age are far more sophisticated than those that were sufficient to get by a few years go. If you're an experienced professional salesperson, part of the danger is that you might not unlearn habits from the past and then learn the new skills you need.

The opportunity lies in the fact that if you understand and implement an effective set of principles and processes, you'll be far more successful than your bewildered competition. You will be equipped for a lifetime of success in the permanent white water of the Information Age.

The Six Hats of the Information Age salesperson will enable you to avoid the danger and take advantage of the opportunity.

2

INTRODUCTION TO
THE SIX HATS

My first professional sales position began with six weeks of intense sales training, and during the training period I lived in a hotel in Mill Valley, California with five other salespeople. We spent eight hours a day presenting a memorized pitch in front of a video camera, and then critiquing one another until we were able to present it perfectly. We learned how to sell that product.

A few years later, in another sales position, I spent another six weeks in training, this time on the east coast, in New York City. The products were different, but the drill was similar: Learn the pitch and memorize the right words for all the anticipated situations. Learn them word for word, and you'll be well on your way to sales success.

That way of training salespeople and the approach to selling that it generated worked well then, but it doesn't work anymore. There was a time when a professional salesperson could "learn the pitch." There was a formula for selling any product or service. Focus on the product, learn the presentation, apply it consistently, and you could be successful.

The focus was on the product and the presentation. The concept was that our product was so unique, so full of features, that all we had to do was accurately describe them to you, and you'd have to buy! Sales success was a matter of memorizing predetermined sets of words for a finite number of situations.

Most sales literature expounded upon the same concept. Learn these twenty-four special closes, and you'll be successful! Memorize these fifteen magic bullets! Use these special words! The preponderance of what passes as sales training today is merely information about products or services, or pat answers and magic bullets from sales gurus who generalize from their limited experience in their industries.

Those types of approaches to sales worked well when we lived in a slower, less competitive age. You really could identify the two or three most common objections for your product and memorize the most effective responses. But, as we learned in Chapter 1, those days are gone!

The world is changing more rapidly than ever. Today's pitch is obsolete tomorrow and memorized solutions, like high-tech products, are obsolete in a matter of a few months. As soon as you master the formula, something changes—the situation, your customer, the competition, or your own product or program. Focusing on the product and the presentation leads to frustrating obsolescence. Searching the literature for packaged solutions is a never-ending journey through a maze. Applying a single sales approach to a constantly changing customer base is ineffective.

Salespeople need a new approach for the Information Age, an approach to their profession that will allow them to change with the environment. That's what *The Six-Hat Salesperson* is all about. If you rely on memorized pitches, magic "closes," and single approaches, you limit yourself to a finite number of situations. It's more important to master certain principles you can apply to countless numbers of situations, and to master certain processes you can use to create your own pitches and identify your own solutions. If you focus on principles and processes you can use to create your own solutions, you'll be equipped to deal with any situation that comes up, no matter how frequently the dynamics of the situation change.

You've heard the saying, "Give a man a fish, and you feed him for a day. Teach him how to fish and you feed him for a lifetime." The same concept applies to selling. Memorize the pitch, focus on the product or the presentation, rely on one way of selling, and you may be successful for a moment. Focus on the underlying principles and processes and you'll be successful for a lifetime.

Many salespeople, for example, have to contend with selling a continuous stream of new products. It's an Information Age challenge. Product life cycles are growing shorter and companies, to stay competitive, churn out upgrades, new products, and new technologies at an accelerating pace. As soon as you master one product or presentation, it becomes obsolete. How do you keep up? Put on the hat of Master Learner and learn to learn more quickly and effectively. *The Six-Hat Salesperson* will show you how to do that, equipping you with effective principles, processes, and tools to make the task easy.

Imagine that you're on the road making sales calls, and you have six different hats arranged on the back seat of your car: Astute Planner, Trusted Friend, Master Learner, Effective Consultant, Skilled Influencer, or Adept Human Resources Manager. When you put on each hat, you magically gain a unique set of abilities. You select hats and combinations of them according to the ever-changing circumstances you encounter. Thus, the hats provide you the power to be successful in a limitless number of sales situations. You can get by without them, but the special insights and abilities you gain by using them enable you to accelerate your sales success. That's the idea underlying *The Six-Hat Salesperson*.

Each of the hats represents a set of competencies. A competency is an area of activity that is important to your overall success. It's an aspect of your job in which, if you're going to be at all effective, you must gain a certain minimum level of proficiency. If you're going to reach success at a level higher than most, then you must continually improve in each of those aspects of your job.

Let's imagine, for example, that you're a professional basketball player. You understand there are certain aspects of the game in which you must have a minimum level of proficiency. You must be able to dribble, to pass, to shoot, to rebound, to defend, etc. Each of these aspects of the game are competencies. They are shared by everyone in the game, no matter what the level. Elementary school children playing basketball can all shoot, dribble, pass, rebound, defend, etc. The difference between them and Michael Jordan is the degree of expertise in each of those competencies.

A competency is made up of a combination of principles, processes, and tools. You gain the magic of the hat by first understanding the principle, and then developing your competency in that area by implementing the associated processes. Eventually, as you become proficient in each of the competencies represented by the hats, you develop a set of almost magical abilities. While you can become skilled at a competency, you never become as good as you can be. In the quest for continuous personal improvement, there is no finish line.

The key to the power of the six hats is understanding the principles and processes involved in gaining mastery of that aspect of your job. According to Webster's, a principle is, "a fundamental truth, law, doctrine, or motivating force upon which others are based." If you understand the principles that support each competency, you'll be able to apply that competency to a continuously changing set of circumstances. Many of the Six-Hat principles will appear to be commonsense observations, and they may be. I've found that the most powerful sales principles are those that are the most easily understood and accepted. The trick is to apply that insight or truth to the salesperson's task.

The principles presented here are based on observations I've made along the way and tested in literally hundreds of sales training sessions with tens of thousands of salespeople around the world. Some of them mark watershed events in my life. In several cases, my discovery of a principle changed the course of my career.

Principles are powerful. Don't let the sometimes simplistic nature of them fool you into underestimating their potential effect on your career.

It's not enough to understand the principles. If it were, all you'd need to be a successful salesperson would be a college degree in sales. Knowledge of principles is necessary, but not sufficient. You need some way to apply those principles to the challenges you face. That's where processes come in. Processes unleash the power of your potential by providing you with a way to implement the principles.

The dictionary defines process as "a particular method of doing something, generally involving a number of steps or operations." Think of a process as a "how-to." It's the missing link in most sales training, the key that unlocks the power of a principle. Combine a principle with a process, and you'll be powerfully equipped.

For years I've held a position that is outside the mainstream thinking of most motivational speakers, success gurus, and sales trainers. It is: *Goal setting is overrated!* Don't misunderstand. I believe in goal setting, and it is described as an integral process in Chapter 4. But as far as being a sure ticket to leading a full and satisfying life, goal setting is overrated. The best things in my life have come to me not as a result of setting goals and working toward them, but rather as a result of adhering to certain principles and processes.

For example, I never set out to find someone to marry. Yet my wife, Coleen, is certainly one of the best parts of my life. I met and developed a relationship with her as a result of taking a risk and attending a Parents without Partners meeting. It was the principle, *It's a good idea to associate with people in the same situation as yourself,* that drove me to seek out a support group and that led to my meeting her.

Our daughter, Kelly, is certainly one of the best parts of our lives. Yet we did not set out to adopt an infant. Rather we followed the principle, *It's more blessed to give than to receive,* became foster parents, and eventually opened our home to a child who later became a permanent addition to the family.

I could go on and on. My career, my spiritual relationships, all the best parts of my life came as a result of adhering to principles and implementing processes, not as a result of setting and working at goals. Principle and processes, therefore, are the keys to this system.

The third component of a competency is the set of tools you need to implement the processes and principles. A tool is anything you use to help you accomplish your job. Computers, cell phones, sales literature, forms, worksheets, and samples are all examples of tools.

Let's apply these three components to the expression, "Give a person a fish, and you feed him for a day; teach him to fish, and you feed him for a lifetime." What does it mean to "teach someone to fish?" It's a matter of principles, processes, and tools.

If you're going to learn to fish, you first need to understand some principles. "Fish eat worms" is a principle. Upon that principle you can build a process. Because "fish eat worms" you can learn to find worms, you can learn to put the worms on a hook, and you can learn to place that hook in the water near where a fish should be. Those are the processes, the how-to's that make up the competency of "fishing."

Finally, your efforts to fish will be significantly enhanced if you have effective tools. Everything else being equal, the person with the sharp hooks, strong line, sensitive rod, and quality reel will do better than the person with a cane pole and a rusty hook. The difference in the results is a function of the tools.

Put together powerful principles, effective processes, and quality tools, and you'll catch fish. It's only when the principle is combined with the process and enabled by good tools that the desired result is obtained—a fish is caught. All three pieces, together, make up the competency of "fishing." If you want to be a master fisher, you need to learn the principles, master the processes, and acquire the tools. Then you'll eat well for the rest of your life.

That's the idea behind *The Six-Hat Salesperson*. Understand the principles, learn the processes, use the tools, and you'll be successful for a lifetime. It's a matter of learning to wear the six hats.

To identify the components of each hat in the text, we've included graphic icons.

⚓ When you see the anchor icon, you'll know that we're discussing a principle. The anchor on a sailboat stabilizes the entire ship and all its occupants; our principles are the anchors that hold the processes steady.

➤ When you see the arrows icon, you'll know that you're learning a process—a step-by-step series of actions that show you how to apply the principle. These cornerstone principles and processes are the heart of *The Six-Hat Salesperson*.

⊤ When you see the tool icon, you'll know that we're discussing a tool to use in mastering that hat.

When you understand the principles and become adept at the processes and comfortable with the tools, you'll be able to succeed in a countless number of situations, with an unlimited number of people. You'll be equipped to succeed in the Information Age.

The Six Hats

When you think about all the challenges that impact a salesperson's performance, you can categorize them into two basic areas: the need to influence the customer and the challenge to manage yourself. In the first six months of my first full-time outside sales position, I came to realize that my success depended on my ability to do both well. No matter how slick I was in my face-to-face interactions with my customers, if I hadn't organized and motivated myself to be in front of the right customers with the right attitude and fully prepared, it didn't matter. I concluded that I had to become good at both sides of the salesperson's challenge.

The six hats are organized to address those two areas. Figure 2-1 depicts that organization.

The first hat, *Astute Planner*, bridges the gap between those two major areas of the salesperson's challenge: working with customers and managing yourself. In the Information Age, you can't afford to dissipate your time; you must become more effective by mastering the discipline of thinking about what you do before you do it—in other words, planning. This competency describes how to focus on your highest-potential customers, plan for key account

FIGURE 2-1

The Salesperson's Challenge

Influence the Customer   Manage Yourself

Friend   Consultant   Influencer   Planner   Human Resources Manager   Learner

The Six Hats

strategies, develop sales call plans, and organize your time by creating daily, weekly, and monthly plans.

The second hat, *Trusted Friend,* describes the competency of creating trusting relationships with customers. In a high-tech world full of confusing choices, people (your customers) are hungry for relationships with competent people they can trust. The Information Age demands a more relationship-oriented approach to sales, and this hat provides specific techniques and processes for making good first impressions, finding common ground with almost anyone, understanding and reflecting individual behavior styles, and operating under a strict code of ethics.

The third hat, *Effective Consultant,* focuses on the competency of being seen by your customer as a valuable consultant. This competency is built upon the principles of knowing the customer more effectively than anyone else does and matching the products, programs, and services you sell to the deeper needs and interests of the customer. No more features and benefits selling; you must identify problems and opportunities and match them to custom-crafted solutions. When you master this hat you know how to understand the customer more deeply, more broadly, and more specifically, to design your presentations and proposals more effectively, and to leverage every transaction into deeper relationships.

The fourth hat, *Skillful Influencer,* teaches the process approach to selling and provides specific strategies and tactics for making powerful presentations, closing the sale, and handling objections.

The fifth hat, *Adept Human Resources Manager,* describes strategies and techniques for managing your greatest resource: yourself! Organizing your files, managing information, applying strategies for time management, overcoming rejection and depression, setting goals—all of these are skills for wringing the most out of your potential.

Finally, the sixth hat, *Master Learner,* describes lifelong learning and continuous improvement, provides six specific strategies to pursue, and describes our unique Menta-Morphosis personal learning system.

3

THE FIRST HAT:
ASTUTE PLANNER

Start with Information

Most salespeople love to be active—out in our territories, seeing people, solving problems, putting deals together. Activity orientation is one of the characteristics of a sales personality. Spending a day sitting behind a desk is our idea of purgatory. Unfortunately, activity orientation is both a strength and weakness. Much of our ability to produce results has its genesis in our activity orientation. It provides some of the energy to move us to sales success. But it can also be a major obstacle. Far too often, we're guilty of going about our jobs in a "Ready, shoot ... aim" pattern. This kind of unfocused activity is a casualty of the Information Age. As a Six-Hat Salesperson, you understand that to be effective you must be focused and thoughtful about everything you do. Activity without forethought and planning is a needless waste of time and energy.

The most important part of your job is the time you spend in front of your prospects and customers. Of all the different parts of your job, there is nothing more important to think about, nothing more important to plan, than that.

If you were to make a list of everything you do and then consider each of the items on the list, you'd likely discover that almost everything you do can be done cheaper or better by someone else within your company. Someone else can call for appointments cheaper or better than you can. Someone else can check on back orders better than you can. Someone else can fill out a price quote, write a letter, or deliver a sample cheaper or better than you can. In fact, it's likely that the only thing you do that no one else in your company can do cheaper or better than you can is interact with your customers. It's the face-to-face interaction with your customers that defines the value you bring to the company. If it weren't for that, your company would have little use for you.

The face-to-face interaction with your customer is the core value you bring to your company, the reason for your job. Yet, most studies indicate that the average outside salesperson spends only about 25 to 30 percent of the working week actually face to face with customers. In light of that, doesn't it make sense to spend some time planning and preparing to make that 30 percent of your work the highest quality you can possibly make it? Of course it does.

That brings us to hat number one—Astute Planner. The Six-Hat Salesperson puts on the first hat and strives to plan and prepare all the important aspects of the job, investing approximately 20 percent of the work time planning and preparing for the other 80 percent.

The Planning Principles

Mastery of this hat is built upon several powerful principles. Here's the first one:

⚓ *Good decisions require good information.*

It's the Information Age, remember. That means that if you're going to be an effective Six-Hat Salesperson, you must collect, store, and use good information. You can't make effective plans if the information on which you build those plans is faulty or sketchy.

If you were going to build a home, for example, you'd want to know about the nature of the ground on which the home was to be built. You'd need to have a good idea about what kind of weather conditions the home would endure, what the building codes were, what materials were available and what they cost, and what kind of skilled workers were required. The list could go on and on. The point is that you wouldn't be able to build a home very effectively if you didn't have good information on which to base your plans.

The same principles apply to building a home and to delivering effective sales performance. In both cases, *good planning requires good information.* It may be that your company provides you with all the information you need, but more likely it doesn't. If you're going to work with good information, you must be the one who collects that information. That means that you must create systems to *collect, store,* and *use* the information that will be most helpful to you. Because our world is constantly producing new information, the system you create isn't something you set up once and forget. Rather, it has to be a dynamic system that is constantly processing, storing, and using new information.

THE INFORMATION COLLECTING PROCESS

Creating and maintaining your system is a matter of following several specific steps. Here's the process:

1. Create a list of the categories of information you'd like to have.
2. Working with one category at a time, brainstorm a list of all the pieces of information you'd like to have within that category.
3. Develop a system and some tools to help you collect that information.
4. Store it efficiently.
5. Use it regularly.

Step 1. Start by listing the kinds of information you think will be most useful to you. Think about your job and determine what kinds or categories of information you'd like to have to help you deal effectively with your customers. Here's a partial list that would fit most salespeople:

- Information about your customers and prospects.
- Information about your competitors.
- Information about the products, programs, and services you sell.

You may have a number of other categories, but this is a basic list you can begin with.

Step 2. Think about what information would be ideal to have in each category. Start at the top and work down. Look at customers and prospects first. What, ideally, would you like to know about them?

Some typical pieces of information would include information about the account's total volume in the kind of products you sell, the dates of contracts that are coming up, the people from whom they are currently buying, and so forth. All of that seems pretty basic. However, most salespeople have no systematic way of collecting and storing that information. So, while you may occasionally ask a certain customer for parts of it, you probably aren't asking every customer for all the information. And you're probably not collecting it, storing it, and referring to it in a systematic, disciplined way.

Do you think your competitors know exactly how much potential each of their accounts has? Do you think they know other pieces of useful information, for example, how many pieces of production equipment each customer has and the manufacturer and year of purchase of each piece? Probably not. If you collect good, quantitative marketing information, you'll be better equipped to make strategic sales decisions and create effective plans. For example, you'll know exactly who to talk to when the new piece of equipment from ABC manufacturer is finally introduced. You'll know who is really ripe for some new cost-saving product that's coming or the new program your company is putting together.

You may currently be doing a so-so job of collecting information. It's like playing golf. Anyone can hit a golf ball, but few can do it well. Anyone can get some information; few salespeople do it well. Doing it well is one indication of mastery of the first hat.

Step 3. Develop a system and some tools. The single most effective tool is an account profile form. It's an incredibly effective tool that generates and organizes some of the most powerful processes.

An account profile form is a form full of questions, or more precisely, spaces for the answers to questions. The questions are all about each of your accounts. The form is the document on which you store that useful information. It can exist in either paper or electronic form. If you're using contact management software on a laptop computer, then the account profile form can be several screens for each account. If your contact information is not computerized, then it needs to be created on paper. Regardless of the media, the principles and processes are the same.

A well-designed, systematically executed account profile form can be one of the most powerful tools for acquiring a competitive edge. It provides you with a way to collect quantitative information that will allow you to know your customers more thoroughly than your competition does. All the pieces of information that you decided were potentially important to you can be collected and stored in the blanks on the account profile form. Create a one-page form with blanks on it for each of the quantitative pieces of information you want to collect.

In addition to the form for quantitative information about the business, you need another version of the form for each of the key individuals within those account companies. That's called a personal profile, and it is your mechanism to collect personal information about the key decision makers. You apply the same concept and principles to the task of collecting personal information about the key decision makers within your accounts. You might end up with one document for the company and ten to fifteen personal profiles for the key people within that company.

Now, imagine getting ready for the next sales call to that company; reviewing the hobbies of the key people and refreshing your memory on their spouses' names, and the names and schools of each of their children. As you plan your presentation, you review the primary buying motivation for each of those key people. Do you think you'll be better prepared to have an enjoyable, relationship-building conversation with that customer than your competitor will? Of course you will. Do you think you'll increase the likelihood of your delivering a powerful and persuasive presentation? Of course you will.

Finally, the form allows you to store important information someplace other than in your head. The problem with keeping information in your head is that it isn't always readily accessible. When you want to have a relaxed conversation with your customers about their interests, you can't always remember that she golfs or that he was a starting halfback on his college football team. However, if you have that information stored on a form, you can review it just before you go in to see your customer and put it uppermost in your mind.

To some degree, every good salesperson implements these concepts. The difference between run-of-the-mill salespeople and Six-Hat Salespeople, however, is the degree to which Six-Hat Salespeople discipline themselves to stick to a systematic approach. Most salespeople collect information as they think of it, but don't store the information systematically. Masters of the Six Hats understand the need to discipline themselves and thus do a more thorough job of collecting information.

Step 4. Store it efficiently. You may have done a great job of collecting information, but if you've stored it on old matchbook covers, coffee-stained Post-it notes, and the backs of old business cards somewhere in the backseat of your car, it's probably not going to do you much good.

If your contact system is computerized, then your computer can be the supertool that allows you to store the information efficiently. Otherwise, you're going to need to create a set of files (yes, manila folders!) in which to store your information. More on this later.

Step 5. Use it regularly. Before every sales call, review the information you have stored. That review will help you make good decisions about each aspect of the sales call. Likewise, review the information when you create your annual goals and sales plans, when you create account strategies, and when you organize and plan your territories.

As you can tell, an account profile form is a master tool that holds all of this together. If you're going to achieve mastery of this hat, you'll need to create this tool. To help you with this most important task, here's a seven-step process for creating your own account profile form.

ACCOUNT PROFILE PROCESS

Step 1. Identify each of the markets to which you sell. You may sell to several different kinds of customers. Each different type of business should have its own version of the form. For example, I sold to hospitals, large outpatient clinics, and independent

laboratories. The differences between these institutions were enormous; each had a different business structure, set of needs, and decision-making apparatus. So each warranted a unique account profile form.

Step 2. Create a list. Begin the form by first listing all the things you'd like to know about your account. For example, you might find it useful to know the number of employees, the SIC code, which competitors are currently involved with the account, who the customer's customers are, what products they manufacture or what services they offer, and so on. The key is to determine the information that is *useful* to you.

Next, create page two, which is the personal profile. This is the form on which you store information about the individuals within each account company. You might have one account profile and several personal profiles for the key decision makers and influencers within the company. List all the things that you'd like to know about each individual decision maker, influencer, or gatekeeper within that account. This is generally personal information such as where they went to school, their interests and hobbies, who you may know in common, the organizations to which they belong, and similar information. Take several days to develop an exhaustive list, writing down ideas as they come to you.

Step 3. Edit the list. Now edit your list of ideas down to those pieces of information you consider most useful. You probably can't collect everything, so collect the information that is most useful. Start with the basics—name, title, and so on—and add the important business information, like how much of each of your product categories that account purchases each year, what kind of business it is, and what the reporting relationships and decision-making processes are.

Step 4. Design the form. Now create the form with spaces for the answers to each of the questions you listed above. Don't get too

involved in creating a perfect-looking document. No matter how thorough a job you've done, you'll probably revise the form in a few weeks, after you have some experience working with it. Design something that is workable for now, and let your day-to-day use suggest the fine-tuning adjustments you'll make along the way.

If you're working with a computer and a contact management program, you might still want to start with a paper form. After you're confident that you have all the right pieces of information, you can then incorporate it into the contact management system. This approach can save you hours of frustration later.

Step 5. Implement the form. Begin to use the form to collect information on every sales call. This doesn't mean that you sit down with pen in hand and interrogate every customer, although a little of that is appropriate. You can collect the information on the account portion in a formal session. Generally, your customers will be favorably impressed with your professionalism and thoroughness.

The formal approach will not work for the personal portion. For this piece, you'll need to review the form before each sales call, solidifying in your mind the information you already have and determining what you need. Then, in the course of the conversation, attempt to listen specifically for those pieces of information that you're still lacking. Completing the form may take six months of sales calls.

Step 6. Refine the form. Review your master form from time to time and revise it as you gain experience with it. You'll soon determine what information is impossible to collect and what really isn't useful. If you're using a computer system, wait until this step of the process to load the form into your contact manager.

Step 7. Refer to the form. Store your forms where you can easily retrieve them each time you call on an account. I suggest you create an account folder for each customer and keep your forms in it. Refer to them before every sales call. By reading over the per-

sonal information you've stored on the form, you'll have it fresh in your mind and you'll be much more likely to work it into a conversation. All of your efforts to create the form and collect information will be wasted if you don't use it before every sales call.

Remember also to refer to the account information when you're doing your planning. As you know, you can't create good plans without good information. The first step in gaining mastery of the Astute Planner hat is to create a system to collect, store, and access useful information.

COLLECTING INFORMATION ABOUT YOUR COMPETITORS

Now that you have a system in place to provide good information about your prospects and customers, you need to turn your focus to another area of your business—your competitors. Information about your competitors can be almost as important as information about your customers. As things change at an increasing rate, it's more important than ever for you to be aware of what your competitors are doing so you don't get blindsided or seriously outmaneuvered.

It happened to me. To this day, I still get a sick feeling in my stomach when I remember the day I lost my largest account to my archcompetitor. It was an account that made up 20 percent of my total volume. In my blissful ignorance, I was content to grow my business by calling on the end users and the purchasing department, while my competition was successfully building a relationship with the administration. The result? My best account signed a prime vendor, sole-source agreement with my competitor, and within sixty days I was almost totally out of that account. I had been blindsided.

That's a lesson that sticks with me, and one from which you can learn. To become good at knowing what your competition is up to, begin by thinking of yourself a little differently. Here's a simple three-step process for mastering this part of the Astute Planner competency.

Step 1. Collect bits and pieces of information. Begin by consciously collecting little bits and pieces of information at every

opportunity. For example, you may have lost a bid or a particular piece of business to your competitors. Rather than moping about it, use it as a learning opportunity. Try to find out from your customers why they awarded the business the way they did. If it was based on price alone, try to find out how much lower the price was. If it was based on something else, find out what. That information won't help for that particular piece of business, but it might give you an insight into the pricing policies or sales strategies of your competition. Write the information down on a 3- × 5-inch card, a piece of scrap paper, or a Post-it note.

Take your good customers to lunch and casually steer the conversation in such a way as to learn something about your competition. Keep your eyes open to the comings and goings of competitive salespeople. Note when you see them and at what account company. Be sensitive and aware of competitive literature, business cards, and price quotes lying around. Don't forget to talk with the other salespeople who work for your company to get their insights.

These are all ways to collect bits and pieces of information. By themselves, they won't help much. But if you combine these bits and pieces, you may very well notice trends, uncover strategies, and discover tactics your competition is using.

Step 2. Store the information. As you collect each bit of information, capture it by writing it down and putting the note in a manila folder marked "Competition." You might even designate a separate folder for each major competitor. If your files are automated, type the information into your computer and store it in either a word processing or a database file.

What you're doing is assembling a quantity of information. Diligently collect those bits and piece of information and file them away.

Step 3. Use the information. After you have collected a quantity of information, you'll be able to open that file on a regular basis, consider all the pieces of information, and discover a great deal about your competitors.

The trick is to collect and store information consistently. Eventually you'll assemble an accurate picture. It's like the popular game show, *Wheel of Fortune*. When Vanna White turns over one letter, it doesn't give you much of a picture of what the answer is. But after she's turned over several of those small individual pieces, the whole becomes clear and the answer to the riddle is simple to understand. That's the way collecting information about your competition works.

The back of an old business card on which you noted that you saw a competitive salesperson showing a new line of widgets, by itself, doesn't mean much. But if you filed that along with all the other bits and pieces of information you've collected, and then pulled it all out and analyzed it, you might see an entirely different situation. Suppose you reviewed that business card note and combined it with the note you made to yourself that you saw some sales literature on the competitive widget line on the desk of one of your client purchasing agents, and then remembered that you lost a major bid to the competition because they quoted a new line at lower that traditional prices. All at once you've uncovered a potential threat to your business. Clearly, your competitor is pushing a new, lower-price widget line. You didn't learn that from any one piece of information, but rather from the combination of all those pieces considered as a whole.

The key to uncovering that information, to discovering what your competition is up to, is to consistently collect pieces of information, store them, and then analyze them as a whole from time to time.

As you may be able to tell, this chapter focuses on skills that previously were not in the toolbox of the typical outside salesperson. In the Information Age, much of your ability to make good decisions depends on your being able to collect good information. You've got to see yourself as a dealer in information as well as a seller of stuff. The first step in gaining mastery of the Astute Planner hat is to get good at collecting useful information.

4
ASTUTE PLANNER: PART II

Now that you've begun the process of collecting, storing, and using good information, you can get serious about planning for your sales success. To do so, you'll need to master some additional principles and processes. Here's the next key principle for mastery of this hat:

⚓ *You'll always be more effective if you think about what you do before you do it.*

I recall going to see a well-known speaker and author give a two-hour presentation.

The auditorium was filled with several hundred people who had paid to learn from this man's insight and wisdom. Early in his presentation, he remarked that he really didn't know what he was going to say and had not prepared anything, that he would rely on the dynamics of the immediate situation to select his thoughts and words. I grew angry. What arrogance! What followed was something of a disjointed, stream-of-consciousness monologue that prompted most of the audience to go away having learned nothing.

If that speaker had gathered some information about the size and demographics of the audience, if he had organized his presentation in an easily understood format, if he had prepared handouts to visually support his verbal presentation, if he had searched his memory for examples and illustrations that would have resonated with this audience, if he had spent some time meeting individuals before the presentation, if he had interviewed some of the audience by telephone beforehand—if he had done any or all of these things, his presentation would have been far more effective.

That's an easy conclusion for us to reach. Of course he would have been far more effective, of course his audience would have gained much more, of course he would have influenced some people to want to hear him again if he had taken the time to prepare the presentation.

Of course it's always more effective to think about what you do before you do it. Can you imagine a football team not creating a game plan or not practicing before the big game? Can you image a musician not preparing a piece of music before the recital? Can you image a politician not practicing the big speech, or a doctor not reviewing the x-rays and the procedure prior to a major surgery, or a lawyer barging into a case without having planned for it? The answer to all of these questions is, "Of course not." In every event of any importance at all, professional, effective human beings plan and prepare beforehand. It's an essential step toward success.

The same holds true for salespeople. If we think about what we do before we do it, providing we think about it in the right way, we'll significantly improve our performance. Unfortunately, many salespeople have the same mind-set that provided the speaker in our example with an excuse for his lack of concern and preparation: Our intuition and incredible spur-of-the-moment, ad-lib skills will get us by. *Wrong!*

You have a great treasury of wisdom and insight that you've acquired through a rich set of life experiences. Much of that wisdom and insight can be directly applied to your sales job, if you will only tap into it and use it. Of course you'll be able to tap into some of that accumulated expertise on the spur of the moment; but you'll be far more effective if you take the time to tap into it before you get into the situation.

If you're going to master this hat, you'll think about what you do before you do it. You'll think about every telephone call, every sales call, every customer, every presentation, every interaction with your customers and prospects. Yet it's not enough to think about what you do before you do it; you must also think about things in the right way. The next section describes how to do that.

⚓ **Good planning is a matter of asking yourself the right questions and then answering them with detail and precision.**

An amazing thing happens when you ask yourself questions— you think of the answers! What sounds so elementary is really a powerful key to unlocking your success. When you ask yourself a good question you stimulate your thinking. For example, you could ask yourself, "What are the three most effective things I could do to improve my sales performance?" That question would prompt you to analyze your performance, determine some possible changes to make in your behavior, and then select the three that appear to be the highest priority. That's a very worthwhile set of thoughts, and they were prompted by the question you asked yourself.

This is only one example, but the principle is incredibly powerful. Learn to ask yourself good questions and you'll think more effectively.

It follows, then, that if you want to think well, you need to ask yourself the best questions. For example, you could ask yourself the question, "What are all the things the customer will not like about me in this upcoming sales call?" Ask that question and your mind will dredge up all the flaws and faults you've filed away in your memory. That's probably not the most effective way to prepare for a sales call. After thinking about that question, you're liable to be depressed and discouraged. Rather, you could ask yourself the question, "What are two or three things I could find out about the customer that would uncover things we have in common?" Think about the answer to that question and your mind will dwell on your customer, not on yourself, and focus on finding common ground in order to build a relationship.

Which of those two questions is the better one for you to ask yourself prior to a sales call? The answer is obvious. But the point is this: If you're going to prepare and plan for your sales interchanges adequately, you need to ask yourself the right questions. When you ask yourself the right questions, you think in the most effective way.

In order to implement this principle, you'll need to master two basic processes. Each of the processes is really a series of questions, asked in a certain sequence. Master these two processes and you'll master the first hat, Astute Planner. You'll gain a competency that will serve you well for the rest of your working life.

The Processes

To implement this principle and acquire the power of the first hat, you'll need to master two processes: the prioritization process and the planning process.

The prioritization process is used to help you make good decisions about where to spend your time, about what to plan. There is just not enough time in the day for you to plan everything. You must first prioritize the things that are important enough to plan. Then you can follow up with the planning process. You'll find that you use the two processes together.

THE PRIORITIZATION PROCESS

This is a four-step process that you can use over and over from now until you retire.

1. **Select the category to be prioritized.**
2. **Identify the outcome.**
3. **Create criteria.**
4. **Apply those criteria.**

Let's apply the four steps to an example.

Step 1. Select the category to be prioritized. Ask yourself, "Of all of these (whatever you're considering), which is the most important?" There are a number of areas that you may want to prioritize, each of which is a separate aspect of your job. For example, if you sell a wide variety of products, you could prioritize the products in order to select those that have the highest priority for you to pursue. If you have twenty things to do tomorrow, you'd certainly want to prioritize those tasks. As an example, we're going to work with an area that might be the single most important category of your job—your customers.

So step one is easy and relatively simple: Select the category to be prioritized. In our example, we're going to select the category "customers."

Step 2. Identify the outcome you want. Ask yourself, "What should be the end result of this process?" In other words, what do you want to end up with? In this case, let's say that you want to end up with a set of three categories of customers—As, Bs, and Cs. Let's further say that you want the As to be the highest-potential accounts, representing the top 5 to 20 percent of your accounts. You want the B category to contain the middle 30 to 50 percent of your accounts and the Cs to be the lowest-potential 30 to 50 percent of your accounts. You've identified what you want to end up with.

Step 3. Create criteria. Ask yourself, "On what basis should I make that determination?" A criterion is a standard by which you judge something or a benchmark by which you measure something.

In this case, we start out by remembering that we're working on our customers and keeping in mind that we want to end up with three classes of customers. We've got to develop criteria to use to separate those customers into the three categories. I suggest we think in terms of "potential."

Normally, when I ask salespeople to identify their A, B, or C accounts, they pull out a sales report and show me who purchased the most. That's history, not potential. I'm interested in the future, not the past. So I suggest we focus on future potential. That means we've got to determine which customers have the highest potential and which have degrees of lesser potential.

What constitutes "high potential?" From a salesperson's perspective, high potential is the ratio between the likelihood of sales dollars (or income dollars) being generated in return for time invested. You may have a potentially huge account, for example, but because of the philosophy or history of that company, you'd have to invest years to begin to receive any sales dollars in return. That is not a high-potential account, because of the out-of-balance relationship between potential sales dollars and your investment of time. A more likely prospect would be a customer with smaller volume, but one that could be converted relatively easily. In that case, the ratio between sales dollars and time invested is more in your favor.

When you determine high potential, use two criteria. The first is *quantified potential*. Quantified potential refers to the total dollars available from that account. In other words, how much of your product can they buy? Obviously each account has a potential to purchase differing amounts of your product. If you can collect that information accurately and with detail, you'll have a good sense of that account's quantified potential. That's the objective criterion.

But that's only half of the issue. The second criterion is subjective. I call it *potential partnerability*. Partnerability is that subjective feeling you gain about the account's potential to eventually become a partner—a loyal, committed, deeply engaged customer that buys everything possible from you, respects you, and looks out for your best interests. This criterion takes into account the chemistry between the two companies and between yourself and your customers, the philosophy of the account company, the fit between their needs and your offerings, etc. Is the account a price buyer, or is it open to creative proposals from you? Is it a progressive, growing organization? Those are the issues that comprise partnerability. You might have one account that has huge quantifiable potential, but because of the philosophy or personalities of the decision makers has no foreseeable partnerability. That account is not a high-potential account.

Step 4. Apply the criteria. Ask yourself, "What happens when I apply the criteria?" You could apply the criteria in our example this way: On a sheet of paper, create three columns. In the first column, list all of your customers and prospects. In the second column, give each of them a rating of 1 to 100 on their quantified potential. Assign 100 to the account in your territory that could purchase the most of your products or services; assign 1 to the smallest.

After you've rated all your customers and prospects on quantified potential, move on to the third column. In this column, use the same 1 to 100 rating, but this time rate each customer's potential partnerability. A rating of 100 in partnerability indicates an account whose subjective factors are all in your favor. A rating of 1 indicates a customer for whom none of the subjective factors are favorable.

Now add the numbers in the second and third columns. The sum of those two criteria will give you a number you can use to sort each of your customers into A, B, and C categories. Call the top-rated 5 to 20 percent of your prospects and customers A accounts. If you have twenty total customers, you should identify one to four of them as A customers. Remember, these customers represent the highest potential dollars returned for time invested.

Then cull out those that appear to offer a minimal return on time invested. Take between 10 and 60 percent and put them in the C column. Those are the lowest-priority prospects and customers. Finally, put all those that are left over in the B column. They represent the middle group of prospects and customers.

You've just worked through the prioritization process. In doing so, you've prioritized the most salient aspect of your business—your prospects and customers.

Congratulations! Now, you can use that process to prioritize other aspects of your business. Use it to prioritize your prospects, your products, your sales calls, etc. Remember the first principle: *You'll always be more effective if you think about what you do before you do it.* Thinking about where to apply your time most effectively by prioritizing the most important aspects of your job is one of the best things you can do. Put on the first hat and prioritize every important aspect of your job. Then you'll be ready to master the next discipline of the first hat—you'll be ready to plan effectively.

THE PLANNING PROCESS

The planning process is a matter of asking a set of seven questions of yourself, in the correct sequence, and then answering them in writing. The resulting written answers become your plan. You can use this process to plan anything worth planning—your territory, your approach to key accounts, each sales call, your month, your week, etc.

Here are the steps and the seven questions to ask.

Step 1. Start with a goal. Ask, "What's the objective?" Always, the first step in the creation of a plan is the identification of the purpose of the plan. If there is no purpose, why have a plan? The purpose of the plan is your objective.

Regardless of what aspect of your business you're working on—planning a sales call, developing a strategy for a key account, organizing your territory, creating a plan for a new product line—you must begin with an answer to this question.

In order to illustrate each of the steps of this process, we'll identify a situation and then work through it step by step. Let's begin by setting a personal financial goal. While sales is a fulfilling, challenging career, most of us wouldn't be doing it if we didn't get paid. To some extent our sales success is a means to an end, not an end in itself. The end is financial reward. So let's focus on your personal financial goals. Let's say you're going to select an objective to begin the planning process with, and that objective is, "Make $75,000 in the next calendar year."

Step 2. Assess the situation. Ask, "What's the situation?" This step requires you to describe, as accurately as possible, the current situation as it relates to the area you're thinking about.

Let's consider our example objective. You've decided you want to make $75,000 next year. You describe the salient aspects of your current financial situation like this:

> *You have a salary of $50,000. You're paid a commission of 10 percent of all sales above your quota. Last year your quota was $750,000 and you just made it. This year your quota is $850,000. To achieve your goal, you'll need to do considerably better than last year.*

You've just described your situation.

Step 3. Identify the obstacles. Ask, "What will hinder me from achieving the goal?" Identifying obstacles is a powerful step in the planning process. This step alone will give you incredible confidence and positive power to achieve your goal. As always, think the question through in as much detail and with as much precision as possible. The resulting answers to the question form the next step in the planning process.

In the example, let's say that you have identified these obstacles:

- Only three of your current accounts are growing.
- Two new competitors are active in your territory.
- A lot of changes are going on in your market.

Step 4. Identify your strengths and your resources. Ask, "What do I have available to me that I can use to accomplish my goal?" Soberly consider your strengths and your resources. What do you have on your side? Do you have personal skills that you can

apply? Has your company provided you with helpful tools, strategies, or competitive advantages? Is there something working in your favor?

In our example, let's say that you have a hot new product line, a commitment on the part of your credit department to loosen the rules a bit and speed up the credit approval process, and your bosses' verbal assurances that they'll do everything in their power to help you penetrate those large accounts.

Step 5. Create an overall plan. Ask, "How am I going to accomplish my objective?" This step is the heart of the process. Now you must consider the best way to reach your goal, taking into consideration the current state of affairs, the obstacles you must face, and your strengths and assets.

In our example, let's say you write the following plan.

1. *Focus my time on high-potential accounts, expanding the business in A accounts by 50 percent.*
   a. *Get the boss to negotiate with the corporate office for some favorable terms and concessions.*
   b. *Push the new product line aggressively.*
2. *Acquire five new accounts.*
   a. *Use the new product line as a door opener.*
   b. *Get the credit department to approve some of the formerly marginal customers who may be having a difficult time buying from my competitor.*

Step 6. Identify the materials and tools you'll need. Ask, "What will I need?" In this step, identify all the tools and materials you'll need. In our example, for instance, you might say that you need:

1. *Some forms to help identify the highest-potential accounts.*
2. *A list of high-potential prospects.*
3. *All the usual sales aids.*
4. *A bunch of new credit application forms.*
5. *Some literature and samples of the new line.*

Step 7. Create a detailed action plan. Ask, "Specifically what steps should I take?" This step requires you to think very specifically and to create a to-do list that precisely identifies each of the steps you'll need to follow, puts them in sequence, and assigns a deadline completion date for each one.

In our example, we've arrived at a skeleton of the first half of our overall plan. Although the final plan will be more detailed than this, this example outline is designed to illustrate the process simply:

   I. Focus my time on high-potential accounts, expanding the business in A accounts by 50 percent.

     a. Identify who those customers are.

       1. Collect some good information using an account profile form.   *Jan. 15*

       2. Discuss the results with the boss.   *Feb. 3*

       3. Agree on the top 20 percent.   *Feb. 3*

     b. Get the boss to negotiate with corporate for some favorable terms and concessions.   *Feb. 15*

     c. Push the new product line aggressively.

       1. Make appointments to collect info on each product.   *Feb. 15*

       2. Have initial presentations made for each product.   *March 15*

       3. Push forward on demonstrations and evaluations as appropriate.

When you've finished this simple seven-step planning process, you will have created the best plan you're capable of developing. You now have in place a specific strategy for accomplishing your goal, along with a checklist of tasks and dates with which to measure your progress. You created the plan by following the seven-step planning process, asking yourself the questions and answering them in writing. The planning process will work for any aspect of your job. Discipline yourself to use this process and you'll be well on your way to becoming a master of the first hat.

In order to show you how to apply this process to other aspects of your job, we'll focus on some powerful applications.

APPLYING THE PLANNING PROCESS TO A ACCOUNTS

You can and should apply the seven-step strategy development process to every one of your A accounts at least once every three months, but preferably every month. In doing so, you will create a plan for doing the most effective things you can do.

Here's an illustration of how to apply the smart planning process to create a strategy for an A account.

Step 1. What's your objective? I know you want to sell stuff, but that's too general. In the next six months, what specifically would you like to accomplish with this account? Is it to meet two or three of the key decision makers? To successfully introduce a new line? To increase your commodity business by 10 percent? To increase your gross margins by a point or two? Be specific.

Step 2. What's the situation? This question requires you to outline the big picture of the account. What's happening within the organization? What role does your company play? What is this customer trying to do? What changes have occurred recently? What competitors are active with this account?

Step 3. What are the obstacles? Specifically, what's stopping you? Is it a well-entrenched competitor? If so, who is it? To what degree does the competitor have the business? Is the obstacle a less than favorable purchasing agent or department head? Is it a philosophy that exists in the organization? The more detailed and specific you can be with your obstacle analysis, the easier it will be to create an effective strategy.

Step 4. What strengths or resources do you have to help you accomplish the objective? You may have a great relationship with one of the decision makers, or you may have one or two products already in the account. Look at the situation realistically. Do you have anything going for you?

Step 5. How are you going to achieve your objective? This question requires you to outline your basic strategy. Are you going to low-bid the next project? Are you going to take the purchasing agent out to a ball game? What is your basic strategy for achieving your goal?

Step 6. What do you need? This question asks what materials, literature, help, and support you need. Do you need a letter, a copy of an article, some samples, the assistance of a product specialist, or the boss's help? What are the things you're going to need to use to help you accomplish your action plan?

Step 7. What specific steps do you need to take to accomplish the objective? If you're going to meet the corporate executives, you may want to:

- *Get their names from the receptionist.*
- *Ask Pat, your contact, to call them and set up an appointment.*
- *Fax a short introductory note to them, then follow up with a phone call asking for an appointment.*
- *When you get the appointment, collect some information to present the "systems" proposal.*
- *Bring Lee, the sales manager, on the second appointment.*

Note that this is a specific list of exactly what you need to do in order to accomplish the objective you described.

Discipline yourself to ask and answer these questions, in this order, for each of your A accounts. You'll take a giant step forward in working smart.

PLANNING YOUR MONTH, WEEK, AND DAY

Let's say that you've taken a few hours at the beginning of the month to work through plans for each of your high-potential accounts. You've got a stack of twenty pages. What now?

Consolidate all of those decisions into a monthly, weekly, and daily plan. Review your lists of "steps to take" and lay them out as to when in the month you want to accomplish each one. That's a skeletal monthly plan. Then break that down to weekly plans for each week. Finally, at the end of each day, review what you actually did accomplish, add in any new important issues, and create a plan for the next day.

PLANNING FOR SALES CALLS

Here's one more vitally important place to exercise your new competency of the first hat. All the previous planning exists to bring you to this point, where you are thinking about the most effective things you can do with your customers. Let's call that "planning a sales call." The process of planning a sales call is the same one used for the other planning; it's just a little less intense. Think of it as an abbreviated version of the basic planning process. Ask yourself these questions, and use an index card or computer database to capture your bulleted responses.

Step 1. What do you want to accomplish? A plan for a sales call, like any other plan, always begins with an objective. Without it, why make the call? If you set out to accomplish nothing, you'll probably be successful.

Step 2. What's the situation? Jot down a few words summarizing the situation as you best understand it. The process of putting words

in writing will help you think with detail and precision. The more precise your thinking, the more accurate and effective your plans.

Step 3. What agreement do you want to end up with? I believe that every sales call should end with some agreement between you and your customer. If nothing else, you can agree to visit again. The more clearly you define the agreement you want to end up with, the more likely it is that you'll actually reach it.

Step 4. How are you going to do that? List the action steps. Exactly what are you going to do, in what sequence?

Step 5. What do you need to do that? Answer this question by gathering the materials, notes, and information you'll need to accomplish your plan.

I've timed this process for myself and thousands of salespeople in my seminars. It takes an average of two minutes to plan a sales call, if you've done all the other work. Those two minutes spent thinking about a sales call will dramatically increase the effectiveness of the call.

Do this and you'll stay focused on the most effective things you can do with your time. You'll become a master of the first hat—Astute Planner.

Trying on the First Hat

How do you actually fold these principles, processes, and tools into your daily routine? First, let's review the three principles we discussed:

1. *Good decisions require good information.*
2. *You'll always be more effective if you think about what you do before you do it.*
3. *Good planning is a matter of asking yourself the right questions and then answering them with detail and precision.*

We articulated these processes to help you implement the principles:

* Information collecting
* Account profile
* Competitor information
* Prioritization
* Planning

So, where to begin? Start with information. If your company has an account profile tool, begin to use it with more detail and diligence. If the company doesn't have one, then immediately begin to develop your own version or discuss the need for one with your sales manager. You can begin to write a rough draft of your form in an hour or two. Why not do it tonight and begin to experiment with using it tomorrow? That's a good start.

As long as you're thinking about information, in the next few days label a manila folder with the word "Competitors" and put it on the front seat of your car, where you'll notice it from time to time. That will remind you to begin collecting those bits and pieces of information and storing them in the file.

One more thing you can do almost immediately is to start planning every sales call by using the planning process.

Those three activities will get you into this hat quickly, with a minimum of hard work and a great likelihood of seeing immediate results. Spend a couple of weeks ironing out the details and turning those behaviors into habits.

When you've collected sufficient information, you'll be ready to move to the prioritization and planning processes. You really need to set aside a full day or two in a mini-retreat in order to focus your time and attention on accomplishing those tasks. Once you get on the other side of that project, you'll find yourself working far more effectively—not harder, but smarter. That shouldn't surprise you. After all, you're now wearing the first hat, Astute Planner.

Wearing the First Hat

When you've fully mastered the principles, processes, and tools associated with the first hat, you'll be operating with forethought in all the important aspects of your job. You'll be systematically and continuously collecting good information about your customers and your competitors. It won't be an isolated event, but a regular part of your everyday routine. Every sales call you make will be an opportunity to learn more about your customers.

Every year, at least once a year, you'll set aside a day or two for a planning retreat. At that time, you'll create goals and plans for the year. You'll review all your accounts and prospects, prioritizing them into A, B, and C categories. You'll develop annual strategic plans for your key accounts.

Every quarter, you'll set aside time to review your progress and make fine-tuning adjustments. You'll think carefully about each of your A accounts and refine your strategic plans for them. You'll review the information in your competitor file, and garner from that an understanding of your competitors' strategies and tactics.

Every month, you'll create written plans for each of your A accounts and consolidate those action steps into an overall plan for the month.

Every week, you'll create plans for the most effective use of your week.

At the end of each day, you'll plan the next day. You'll think about every sales call and every customer contact and create a plan for each of them.

As a result of wearing this hat, you'll become far more effective and rise to the top in your career.

Application: Using the Six Hats to Turn Challenges into Opportunities

Challenge: My customers don't have much time to spend with me.

Your customers used to be able to spend more time with you. But lately it seems that they are on tighter schedules and are harder to see. You just can't spend as much time with them as you'd like because they're pressuring you to move on.

This is a real Information Age issue. You know how confused and pressured you feel these days. Your customers feel the same way. As pressures brought on by rapid change, growing competition, and the need for every organization to become more streamlined and efficient have hit your customers, their organizations have reacted by trying to make their employees more productive. As a result, your customers have too much to do and not enough time in which to do it, just like you. Some of your customers are walking around with day-planners under their arms today when, just a couple of years ago, they didn't know what a day-planner was. Time, more than money, is the precious currency of the Information Age.

It's not that your customers don't like you (although they may not) nor that they are not interested in your products and services. It's just that they have too much to do, and they simply don't have as much time to spend with you as you'd like.

IMPLICATIONS

This development is truly ominous because the implications strike at the heart of your ability to perform for your company. Let's think for a minute about the value you bring to your company. Why do they employ you? What do they really need you and other salespeople to do? If you were to boil it down to its most fundamental level, you'd probably say that your company needs you to create relationships and spend time face to face with your customers.

Anything that interferes with your ability to spend time face to face and person to person with your customers threatens the heart of your job, the core value you bring to your company. That's what makes this challenge ominous. If you can't spend quality time in front of the customer, your days as a salesperson are numbered.

APPLYING THE SIX HATS

First, put on the second hat, Trusted Friend. Remember to respect your customers' time constraints. If you try to overstay your welcome, you'll only succeed in making them more irritated with you. Do unto them as you would have them do unto you. Protect the relationship.

Then put on the first hat, Astute Planner. Focus on making the time that you do have with customers more productive for both of you. Think of the issue being *quality* time, not *quantity* time. Here are three strategies that will work for you.

1. **Focus on the *quality* of the time you have with your customer.** If you're not going to have as much time in front of the customer as you'd like, then you must concentrate on making the time that you do have as valuable and productive as possible. That requires you to spend more time planning and preparing for each sales call.

   Gone are the days when you could just "stop in." Rather, make sure that you have at least three things prepared for every sales call:

   • A specific objective: What do you want to accomplish in this call?

   • An outline of how you're going to accomplish that objective

   • All the necessary tools you'll need to do it

   Use the planning process to make sure that you're spending high-quality time with your customer. That way, the actual time that you spend with your customers will be more productive. Your customers will appreciate your organization and your respect of their time, too.

2. **Set an agenda; talk in terms of the customers' needs.** Begin every sales call with an agenda. Tell your customers what you want to cover and how you're going to proceed. Mention the needs and objectives they're interested in, and explain how you're going to address them. This will relieve

customers of the worry that you're going to appropriate their time unnecessarily, and will allow them to focus on you.

For example, at the beginning of your sales call, you could say something like this:

Terry, I know you're interested in the cost payback of a possible investment in a new telephone system. I'd like to share with you some of the numbers that others have used to investigate this kind of purchase. After we go through these, I'll address any other questions you may have, and then we'll talk about the next step in this process. Does that sound reasonable?

3. **Always have something of value to discuss.** This is a longer-range strategy. As you consistently hold to this principle, over time you'll build up a certain expectation in the customers' minds. Don't expect an immediate payback from this strategy; nonetheless, stick to it for the long haul.

Think of the time that your customers do spend with you as an investment by the customers. Put yourself in their shoes and see the situation from their perspective. Are they gaining something of value from you in exchange for their investment of time? You want the answer to that question to be "Yes."

In order to generate that perception in your customers' minds, make sure that every time you see them, you have something of value to share or to discuss with them, something in which the customers are interested. If you have nothing that the customers will think is of value, don't take their time. Wait to see them until you do have something of value.

After a few such calls, your customers will come to respect you and look forward to your calls. They'll know that you're not there just to work an agenda of yours, and they'll come to expect to gain something from your sales calls.

You'll find it easier to make appointments and get time with your customers when you've built in them the expectation that the time spent with you will be well worth the cost of it.

5

THE SECOND HAT: TRUSTED FRIEND

A couple of years ago I decided to hire a lawn care company to fertilize my lawn. My next-door neighbor had been using the company for a couple of years and his lawn looked significantly better than mine. So I got the name and phone number of the company and called them.

When I spoke to the salesman, I explained my situation and asked what kind of service plans they offered. He told me they would come out and treat my lawn for an introductory price, and then leave a bill in a plastic envelope hanging from my doorknob. I said that was okay, and asked him to leave a written description of their services and options, so that I could review it and then decide what program to sign up for. He said he would, and that I could then cancel anytime I wanted.

At that, I pricked up my ears and grew suspicious. First he said he'd leave the information for me to review, and now he was saying that I could cancel anytime I wanted. "What do you mean?" I asked.

"We'll start you next week, and you can cancel anytime you want."

I said, "Wait a minute, you said you'd leave some literature, and now you're saying that I can cancel anytime. I'm not committing for the summer. I just want to review my options and then make a choice.

He said, "But..."

I said, "That's not how I want to do this."

He said, "But..."

I said, "No!" and hung up.

Let's analyze what happened. I was as ready a buyer as there could be. I knew the company and I had already decided to buy. It should have been a simple, easy transaction. But the salesperson said something that made me suspicious of him. First, he said that he would leave the information for me in an envelope. Then he said that I could cancel at any time, implying that my decision to have them come out the first time was a commitment for a season-long program. That may have been a very reasonable offer, but I saw it as a contradiction. First he told me one thing, and then he told me something that contradicted that. I got a suspicious feeling about the salesperson. I decided that I couldn't trust him. Since I couldn't trust him, I couldn't trust the company.

I knew the company was competent, the service was adequate, the price was fair, and I wanted to buy. What happened? I lost trust in the salesperson and that was reason enough not to buy. The reason the salesperson didn't make the sale had nothing to do with the classic things that we salespeople like to focus on. Rather, it had to do with my feelings about him.

The point of the story? In our rapidly changing world, because it is more and more difficult to distinguish your product and your company from the competition, the role of the relationship between you, the salesperson, and your customer is more important than ever before.

If you're going to be an effective salesperson in the Information Age, you must be competent at building relationships with a variety of different people—your customers. You must be able to cause your customers to see you as a competent person they can trust, someone with whom they are comfortable. That means that you must become a master of the second hat: Trusted Friend.

That doesn't mean that you have to make friends of your customers in the traditional sense of the word, although you may very well do so. It does mean that you understand three aspects of friendship. Friends are *comfortable* with one another, friends *trust* each other, and friends *respect* each other. Then you work with science and discipline to become very good at influencing your customers to *trust* you, to *respect* you, and to be *comfortable* with you. Whether you see your customers for only a few moments or you visit them regularly over the years, you can apply the principles and processes of the second hat.

Learning to use the second hat in every sales interaction will provide you with a powerful competitive advantage. In spite of the Internet, fax machines, E-mail, mailhouse catalogs, telemarketers, pagers, and cell phones, the role of the personal, one-to-one relationship in sales will grow in importance, not shrink. Certainly there will be buyers who prefer the impersonal world of the Internet or who don't mind the inconvenience and time lost due to shopping at the big superstores. But more and more, the mature decision maker will come to rely on a relationship with someone he or she knows and trusts to guide buying decisions.

Why is that? Because of Shredded Wheat! Remember my experience in the grocery store? When faced with a confusing array of choices, too much to do and too little time in which to do it, I resorted to a relationship with a brand I knew and trusted. It was the relationship I relied on.

A natural reaction to a high-tech world is to seek out high-touch relationships. The knee-jerk reaction to a situation of overwhelming confusion and uncertainty is to lean on a relationship with a competent person you know and trust. As their worlds become more and more turbulent, your customers will seek out trusted relationships. The salesperson who can make the customer feel comfortable, who can be seen as a competent person the customer can trust, will gain an advantage. You achieve that position by developing high-touch relationships—turning your customers into friends.

Getting people to see you as competent and trustworthy—a friend—is a competency. Welcome to the second hat, becoming a Trusted Friend. It's based on an incredibly powerful principle.

⚓ *People find reasons to buy from people they are comfortable with, who they trust and respect.*

Look at buying from the perspective of the buyer. Two issues override almost every other consideration: time and risk. Just a few years ago, your customers had more time to invest in buying decision than they do today. In the Information Age, time is one of the most precious commodities. It matters little whether your buyers are individual consumers making major purchases, like autos or expensive new suits, or whether they are making major capital investment decisions on behalf of their organizations. They have less time today to give to those decisions.

The natural reaction to a situation in which you have too little time to devote to a buying decision is to fall back on a relationship with someone (or some company) you know and trust. Remember my Shredded Wheat decision? I could have read every label, looking for the best nutritional combination; or I could have unholstered my calculator and worked out the best value in terms of ounces per cents; or I could have simply taken the cheapest product on the shelf. But I did none of those. Faced with too many things to look at and not enough time, I resorted to a relationship with a brand that I knew and trusted, something I was comfortable with.

"But a brand isn't a person," you're thinking. That's right, but the principle is the same. It's the relationship that saves you time, no matter whether that relationship is with a brand, a company, or a person.

As I'm writing this, I'm preparing to buy a car. I've already decided that I'm going to limit my search to one of the dealers on the main thoroughfare closest to my house. Why? Because I don't want to take the time to drive all over town. Within a three-mile radius of my house is a Toyota dealer as well as Ford, Chevrolet, Dodge, Mercury, and Volkswagen dealers. Is there really anything to be gained by looking at all the other brands? Are they really that different? Probably not. Isn't shopping all the available brands going to be a waste of time? I think so.

Here's an even greater heresy for the automobile executives: I really don't have a preference for a brand. We're going to buy a mid-size sedan. Looked at objectively, is there really much difference between a Camry and a Taurus? Or between the offerings of all those other brands? From my perspective, the features are all about the same and the prices are about the same. Competitive pressures have meant that no one model can get significantly ahead of the others, and no one can price their products too far away from the others' prices. Sound familiar?

Frankly, we'll probably buy from the first salesperson who impresses us as honest, competent, and concerned about our best interests.

Our perspective isn't very unusual. In the overwhelmingly competitive Information Age economy, time is a critical component. A relationship, as evidenced by our perception of the salesperson as competent, confident, and trustworthy, saves us time.

Risk is the other of the two primary issues influencing us to rely on a trustworthy, competent salesperson. It's my belief that, for most buyers, risk is the ultimate deciding factor. It's not the cost in financial terms of a decision; it's the risk. I define risk as the social, psychological, emotional, and financial cost customers must incur if they make a mistake.

Here's an illustration to help you understand this concept. Imagine that your spouse has asked you to pick up a package of disposable cups on the way home from work today because you're having friends over for dessert and drinks tonight. You stop at the local grocery store and make a selection between brand A and brand B. You pick brand A.

When you bring them home, your spouse mixes up a pitcher of margaritas and pours one. The drink leaks out the bottom of the cup and puddles on the counter. There is a hole in the bottom of the cup. You pour your drink into another cup and it leaks, too. In fact, every one of the cups you bought is defective.

What happens to you in this instant in time? What is the consequence of your decision? I don't know about you, but I would be the recipient of some negative emotion. My spouse would be upset at me. That may be the most painful cost of your decision, but there are other costs.

You're going to have to fix the problem. If there's time, you'll need to run back to the store and replace the cups. So in addition to the emotional cost, you must pay in terms of extra time and additional money, all because of your bad decision. You accepted that risk when you made your decision.

Here's a simple exercise to help you understand this concept. Draw a short vertical line. At the top of the line write the number 25. At the bottom, write the number zero. Now on a scale of zero to 25, where would you put the risk of buying a package of disposable cups? It's close to zero.

Here's an example at the other end of the scale. I have an adoption agency as a client. When a young woman has a crisis pregnancy and she's making a decision as to whether to release her unborn child for adoption, how big a risk is that for her? Most people say that it's a 25. There will be a lifetime of consequences for at least four people. That's a very high risk.

The point of this exercise is to see the situation from your customer's point of view. When you ask your prospects to say yes to you, they are accepting some risk. Each decision you ask of them carries with it a different degree of risk. Setting an appointment with you carries one level of risk, taking the time to try out your product carries another, and committing to a multiyear contract is another, greater risk.

Imagine a typical prospect. Then think of the typical offer or decision you ask of that person. Now, put yourself in the prospect's shoes, and see the situation through different eyes. On the zero to 25 scale, how much risk does the prospect accept by saying "yes" to you?

Here's an easy way to calculate it. Just ask yourself what happens to that individual if you or your company messes up. If you don't show up for the appointment or turn out to be a real jerk, your customer has only lost 30 minutes or so. Not a great risk. If the trial of your product turns out to be a failure, you've cost your customer some time and money as well as the time and inconvenience of the other people involved. That's a greater risk. What about the multiyear contract? If your company doesn't fulfill your end of the deal, your customer could lose a job!

You now have an idea of how your customer looks at the buying decision. The greater the risk, the more difficult the decision.

At this point, you're probably thinking, "Okay, so how can I reduce the risk for my customers?"

You know the answer. Build a relationship. Make a friend. Cause your customers to see you as a competent person they can trust, as someone with whom they're comfortable. Relationship mitigates risk. The greater the relationship, the more customers are comfortable with you, the more they trust you, the more confident they are in you, the less is the perceived risk. So we've discovered a powerful selling principle:

Relationships save the customer time and mitigate the risk.

Are you convinced? Good. Then let's look at each of the three aspects of friendship—comfort, trust, and respect—and apply the principles and processes of the second hat. Let's look at the issue of comfort first. Here's the guiding principle:

⚓ **People are most comfortable with people who are like themselves.**

This is such an obvious principle that I'm hesitant to include it. Of course we understand that people are comfortable with people who are like themselves. That's why your friends are people who are your age, with your values and your interests. It's why people who are of the same economic and social status live near one another, belong to the same organizations, and attend the same churches.

The problem is not that we don't understand this principle, but that we don't apply it to our sales careers. Let's think about this a minute. If people buy from people with whom they are comfortable, and if people are comfortable with people like themselves, and if we work with all kinds of people—our customers—then shouldn't we ... *be like our customers*?

Shouldn't we, to the degree that we are able, influence our customers to be comfortable with us by being like our customers?

Whose responsibility is it to make the sale, anyway? Isn't it yours? Then shouldn't you be the one to adjust your behavior, your style, in order to make your customer comfortable with you? Of course.

If I asked you which animal good salespeople are most like, what would you say? Some people think immediately of a lion roaring through the jungle, master of all it sees. Others say a fox, crafty and thoughtful. Still others say a dog, because of a dog's loyalty and likability.

FIGURE 5-1

None of these is my model. I like to think of good salespeople as being like chameleons (see Figure 5-1). You're familiar with the chameleon. It's the lizard blessed with the unique ability to change colors to blend into its environment. If a chameleon is walking through green grass, it's green. If it's running across brown sand, it's brown.

Great salespeople have a similar ability. They reflect the behavioral styles of their prospects and customers. Like the chameleon, they can "change colors" depending on the demands of the environment they find themselves in. I call this skill "reflective behavior." It's the most sophisticated and powerful relationship-building skill.

As a professional salesperson intent on building relationships, being a chameleon means that you take on the style the customer is most comfortable with. If your customer is thoughtful and deliberate, sober and subdued, be the same things yourself. If your customer is quick and assertive, match that style quip for quip.

When I discuss this concept in my seminars, someone often responds with the question, "Isn't that phony?"

The answer is no. Think of yourself as a diamond. You can rotate the diamond to reflect certain facets of yourself that are already there. If you don't have it in you, you can't be something you're not. When you reflect a customer's unique style, you're choosing to reflect and emphasize a certain part of yourself. You're subjugating your own passing emotions by a decision of will to be disciplined in reflecting your customer's behavioral style back to him or her.

We're not talking about issues of substance; we're talking about style. I'm not suggesting that if you're a Republican you pretend you're a Democrat. That's an issue of substance, and to lie about it would be dishonest. Focus on style, not substance.

Occasionally when I'm teaching this concept someone will say, "I have my own style of selling." My response? "Grow up." Your style isn't important. *Your customer's style is.* If you're going to be an effective salesperson in the Information Age, you're going to have to acquire an edge in a competitive world. That means making your customers comfortable with you, and that means reflecting your customer's style at the expense of your own. It's the mature, professional approach.

One more example: When I come home from work and hear my wife talking on the phone, within a moment or two I can tell who she is talking with. It has nothing to do with what she says, and everything to do with how she says it. She uses one mode of communication—tone of voice, expression, etc.—with our oldest son, another with our daughter, still another with our youngest son, and so on. She intuitively understands that the onus for effective communication rests with the communicator.

How do you do it?

You apply this principle by reflecting three of your customer's attributes: communication style, language, and connections.

Communication Style

Everyone has a most comfortable style of communicating with other people. I recall a sales call I made to the regional vice president of a national company. His office was in Fort Wayne, Indiana. I had a difficult time finding the office because I was expecting it to be in a modern office building. After all, he was responsible for all of his company's operations in one-third of the country. Finally I located the address—an old, abandoned grocery store that had not been significantly renovated. It still had the imprint of the grocer's sign on the bricks and the old plateglass windows in the front. As I entered, I noticed that the old tile floor was still in use.

The receptionist directed me into my customer's office. As I entered, I noticed a modular office partition leaning up against the wall on my left. On it was tacked a sales chart. The walls were bare: no decorations, certificates, or photographs to be seen.

In the middle of the office was a metal desk and in front of the desk, two chairs that did not match. The customer was wearing a suit and tie (the suit jacket was buttoned). He looked up as I came in, extended his hand very formally, and said, "What can I do for you?"

Let's reflect on this situation. What kind of communication style do you think this customer is most comfortable with? Before we discuss that, let's look at another example.

This was another sales call I made on a person of a similar position—executive vice president of a company of a similar size in Grand Rapids, Michigan. As I was led into his office by the receptionist, I almost tripped on the carpeting, it was so thick. The corner of the office to my left was decorated with a number of photographs of his sons playing hockey. There were some homemade cards, the kind created in kindergarten classes, saying " I love you, Daddy," and decorated with crudely drawn hearts. Across the back wall was a wooden bookshelf, laden with knickknacks and photographs. There was a rich, dark wooden desk with two matching, thickly upholstered chairs. A sectional sofa hugged the wall across from the desk, and a coffee table with a coffee pot and cups sat in the center of the room.

My customer had on a tie, but his suit coat was hanging on the back of his chair and his sleeves were rolled up. As I entered the office, he came around the desk to greet me, shook my hand, put his other hand on my shoulder, guided me toward the sectional sofa, and said,

"Sit down over here, and let's talk."

What kind of communication style do you think he was most comfortable with?

Certainly not the same style as the Fort Wayne customer. What kind of response would be most appropriate from me, if I'm going to be guided by the principle, *People are most comfortable with people who are like themselves?*

Everything about the environment and the personal appearance of the Fort Wayne customer told me he was a *"director."* That's someone who is very formal, serious, businesslike, task-oriented, and to the point. My job, as a chameleon salesperson, is to reflect that style. When he greeted me with, "What can I do for you?" I responded with, "I have three items on the agenda. Here's the first." I assessed his style and reflected a communication style he was most comfortable with.

On the other hand, everything about the Grand Rapids customer screamed *"socializer"* at me. That's someone who is friendly, very people-oriented, and sensitive to the emotional side of interpersonal communications. When he greeted me by directing me to the sofa, I began the conversation with, "It looks like your kids play hockey, right?" My job was to assess his most comfortable communication style and reflect it.

Could you imagine me sitting down on the sofa and saying to him, "I have three items on the agenda; here's the first one"? Of course not. Regardless of my style, regardless of my agenda, that wouldn't have been his style.

You've got the idea. If you can accurately identify each of your customers' styles, you'll be able to reflect that style when you're with him or her. In doing so, you'll influence your customer to be comfortable with you.

The study of communication style is a science that goes back several decades. A great deal of research has been done on the topic, a number of books have been written about it, and entire companies have been built around the concept.

Almost every author in the field uses a different set of terms to express very similar concepts. For our purposes, let's assume that there are four basic communication styles: the two I've already mentioned, director and socializer, as well as two others, thinker and supporter. Here's a description of the most obvious characteristics of each.

- **Director.** The primary communication need of this type is to dominate or control the interaction. Directors are formal, serious, and task-oriented. They'll tell you things and they get impatient with the details.

- **Socializer.** The primary communication need is to influence. Socializers are very people-oriented, open, and sensitive to others. They like recognition and being with people, and are interested in the emotional component of communication.

- **Thinker.** Their primary motivation is compliance. Thinkers are generally very slow to react, preferring to think things through. They are often formal and conservative in their attitudes and communication.

- **Supporters.** Their primary motivation is steadiness. Supporters are interested in numbers and facts, and are money- and time-oriented. They are the most risk-averse of all the types.

As always, to implement the principle, you'll need to understand and use a how-to process. Here's a simple two-step process to help you.

THE REFLECTIVE BEHAVIOR PROCESS

1. Assess your customer.
2. Reflect your best understanding of his or her style.

Here's how to implement these steps.

Step 1. Assess your customer. Human beings are fascinating creatures who can almost always be counted on to make a mark on their environment. That means that a person's work environment almost always reflects his or her personality. Your job, as a competent Six-Hat Salesperson, is to quickly study your customer's environment so you can pick up clues as to your customer's communication style.

Reflect on the two examples I described above. The complete lack of decoration and the stark functionality of the environment of my Fort Wayne customer told me, before I ever laid eyes on him, that he was a direct, to-the-point, task-oriented person. On the other hand, the warm, comfortable environment and overwhelming number of "people" decorations showed me that my Grand Rapids customer was a people person.

As you initiate a sales call, discipline yourself to quickly study the customer's environment to pick up those kinds of clues. Whenever possible, strive to have the meeting in the customer's personal work space. It won't do you much good, for example, to meet with a customer in a conference room that doesn't reflect your customer's personal presence, when you could have met in his or her office.

Study your customer's personal presentation. By that I mean the manner in which your customer has chosen to appear to you.

Remember my Fort Wayne customer's buttoned-up look and my Grand Rapids customer's sleeves-rolled-up look? Both were indications of their personal presentation.

Finally, assess the customer's actual physical behavior. Body language can be enormously instructional. Mr. Fort Wayne rose rather stiffly and reached across the desk, keeping it between him and me. My Grand Rapids customer came around the desk, greeting me at the door, and put his hand on my shoulder—all indications of a people-person, a socializer.

Here are some clues to help you quickly assess your customer's communication style:

- **Directors.** Stark, functional environment; formal, conservative, "buttoned-up" personal presentation; stiff, aloof, standoffish body language, direct eye contact.

- **Socializer.** Warm, comfortable environment, with lots of evidence of people interests; often trendy clothing, warm personal presentation; close contact, open and sweeping gestures.

- **Thinker.** Often cluttered environment; clothing often looks like an afterthought—doesn't always go together; asks a lot of questions; few hand gestures, not much eye contact.

- **Supporters.** Decorated environment—flowers, cards, etc.; soft, comfortable, and often attractively dressed; nonaggressive body language.

Step 2. Reflect your customer's style. You've done a quick assessment of your customer's most comfortable style. Now it's your job to reflect or match that style. The easiest way to do this is to ask yourself how your customer would like to be dealt with. What sort of style from you would make the customer most comfortable?

For example, if you peg your customer as a director, don't ask about his or her hobbies. That's much too personal. If you deem your customer to be a socializer, don't get right to the point. That's much too task-oriented.

I really can't give you a list of tactics, because people are too different. But I can urge you to be guided by the golden rule of behavior styles: Communicate with your customer in the style your customer is most comfortable with.

Language

We've been discussing the process of reflecting communication styles as a way of making your customers comfortable with you. But communication isn't the only aspect of a customer's style with which you need to be concerned. Focus also on your customer's language. Use the customer's words, expressions, and cadences in talking with him or her, and you'll once again be perceived as being like your customer—someone it is easy to be comfortable with.

I recall a sales call I made to a particularly good client.

"Today in my business," he said to me, "It's like we're stuck in the middle of a fast-moving river, trying to swim against the current of all these small orders we receive every day."

He could have described his business problem by talking about the numbers of orders he received, the overloaded customer service staff, and the backlog at the data-input desk. Instead, he chose to use an analogy.

My response? "It sounds like we should build some water sluices and dams to get control of the flow."

"That's it exactly!" he exclaimed.

I could have said that we needed to create policies and procedures to systematically screen and process those orders. But that would have been my terminology, not his. Instead, I chose to speak in his language, in the style with which he was most comfortable.

That's an example of reflecting your customer's *language*.

Use the same two-step process, but apply it to language as well as communication style.

1. Assess your customer.

2. Reflect your customer's language.

This is a matter of listening not just to what your customer is saying, but also to the actual words and expression.

Listen specifically to your customers' analogies. An analogy is a comparison. My customer in the example chose to speak about his flow of orders by comparing it to the current in a river. Many of your customers have favorite or comfortable analogies. When you explain your product or service in terms of their analogies, they feel that you understand them and you're like them. You've made major steps forward in your attempt to make them comfortable with you.

Listen also to their expressions. People develop expressions and slang that arise out of their experiences and their associations. When you use those same expressions you send the subconscious signal that you can relate to their experience and their environment.

Last year I presented a number of programs in southern Africa. Early in the first program, one of the audience used the expression, "That's a real thumb-sucker." I was dumbfounded. What on earth did that mean? Everyone in the room seemed to accept the comment without hesitation, so I concluded that it must be a common expression. At the break, I asked a group what it meant. When I learned that it meant "something obvious," I used it regularly throughout the balance of my seminars.

Finally, if you really want to become a sophisticated reflective behavior practitioner, listen to your customer's cadences. Cadence is the rhythm of a person's speech. Some people speak slowly, others rapidly. Some accentuate certain parts of a sentence, others don't. Each person has a unique rhythm. Concentrate on picking up on that cadence and using a similar rhythm in your conversation. Remember the two-step process—assess and reflect.

Connections

You've heard the expression, "Birds of a feather flock together." Applied to people, not birds, it means that people who are alike tend to go to the same places, be interested in the same things, join the same organizations, etc.

You're thinking, "So what?" Here's what: The obverse is also true. "If birds flock together, they are probably of the same feather." Applied to people, it means that if people have the same things in common—if they go to the same places, are interested in the same things, join the same organizations—then they are probably a lot alike.

If you want your customers to become comfortable with you by seeing you as like them, then make sure you point out those things (connections) that you have in common with your customers. The more people, places, organizations, and experiences you have in common with your customers, the more they perceive you to be like them.

As you may have guessed by now, you use the same two-step process to implement this concept.

1. **Assess your customer.**
2. **Reflect your customer's connections by mentioning them.**

Study your customer's work environment, personal presentation, language, stories, illustrations, etc., and find some things that you have in common. You may have been to the same place, traveled or gone on vacations to the same area, gone to the same church, rooted for the same sports teams, belonged to the same civic organizations, seen the same movies, read the same books, attended the same plays, or known the same people. Got the idea? The sooner you find something you have in common, the sooner you'll be able to put the prospect at ease and make him or her comfortable with you. After you've found something you have in common, work it into the conversation as early as you can.

Here's a real-life example from my own experience.

I went into a man's office, a CEO of a small business, to meet him for the first time. I was there to discuss sales training. He asked if I wanted a cup of coffee. By the way, I always take a cup of coffee, even if I've just come from a breakfast meeting and have had six cups of coffee already and am beginning to wonder where the rest room is.

There's a reason I do that. Think about what happens when you say, "Yes, I'll have a cup of coffee." Your host has to arrange for it, either getting the coffee or instructing someone else to get it. In either case, it will take a few moments to attend to the task. While your host is doing that, you can use the time to look around the office and find something to be interested in.

That's exactly what happened. When my customer was out making arrangements for coffee, I spotted a large photograph of a sailboat. I sail, so I immediately chose that as the item in which I would be interested, my point of common ground.

When he came in and handed me the coffee, the first thing I did was point at the photograph and ask, "Do you sail?" He replied, "Yes, that's my boat." The photograph was large enough for me to make out the name of the boat, Kelly Ann. I said, "I have a daughter named Kelly Ann." And he said, "*I* have daughter named Kelly Ann. The boat was named after her."

At that point the conversation turned to daughters and sailing, and we achieved a real, common bond based on our similar interests and experiences. None of this would have happened had I not disciplined myself to find common ground.

That brings us to a very special kind of connection you can make with our customers, the connection of one real, live human being to another. The fact is that—when you meet a customer for the first time, particularly in the first few minutes of your visit, he or she tends to treat you as a stereotype. You're a salesperson, not a real person. As long as you allow yourself to be treated as a stereotype, you'll maintain a superficial, stereotypical relationship. You need to make a "real human being" connection with the customer. You need to break through the stereotype and cause your customer to see you as person. You make this connection, breaking though the wall between your customer and yourself, by sharing something unique and personal about yourself.

Here's an example. During the first few minutes of most meetings I have with a new prospect, I try to work into the conversation the fact that my wife and I are foster parents. Over the years, we have cared for eighteen foster children.

You're probably asking what that has to do with sales. My answer is, "Nothing." But if you ask what it has to do with creating a relationship with the prospect, getting myself seen as a real, live human being, then I'd say it has *everything* to do with that.

You see, once I share something unique and personal about myself, that I'm a foster father, the prospect can no longer treat me as a stereotype. I am now a *real* person with *real* blood flowing through my veins. I've connected to the "humanness" in the prospect. You can do the same thing.

Let's summarize. Influencing your customers to be comfortable with you, an essential Six-Hat Salesperson's competency, is a matter of helping them see you as being like them. Your primary process is that of assessing and then reflecting your customers' communication styles, language, and connections.

Now we're ready to work on the other two aspects of the second hat: influencing your customer to trust and respect you.

6

TRUSTED FRIEND: PART II

Gaining Your Customer's Respect

Remember the primary principle anchoring this hat: *People find reasons to buy from people they are comfortable with, who they trust and respect.* You must make your customers comfortable with you, but you must also influence them to respect you (to see you as competent) as well as trust you. When your customers see you as a competent person they can trust, the buying decision becomes less of a risk.

Let's consider the principles and processes for each of these issues, beginning with influencing your customers to perceive you as competent.

⚓ *People perceive you as competent not so much by what you say, but rather by what you ask.*

Did you ever go to a new physician for the first time, only to have her elicit from you an incredibly detailed health history? She puts you through the wringer, inquiring about all the little details of every illness or health incident you've had. By the time you are finished, you are exhausted. You leave the office thinking to yourself, "Wow, was she good."

What made you think that? Was it what she said, or what she asked? Obviously, it was her detailed and knowledgeable questions.

Here's another example: Suppose you're having difficulty with your automobile, so you take it into the mechanic down the street. You notice a neon sign in the window announcing "Computer diagnostics." On the walls of the reception room hang several certificates.

"I'm having trouble with my automobile," you say. "It's making a funny noise."

"We're all certified," he says, "And we have computer diagnostics. Leave the car here and pick it up at 5 p.m."

You aren't totally sold, so you go across the street to the competing mechanic's shop. You notice there is no sign in the window and no certificates on the wall.

You say the same thing to the mechanic. "I'm having trouble with my automobile. It's making a funny noise."

"What kind of noise?" he asks.

"It's a strange thumping sound," you reply.

"Can you describe it?"

"It sounds like something metal banging against something else."

"Where is it coming from?"

"Someplace in the front; sounds like more to the passenger side of the car."

"What kind of car is it?" he asks.

"A 1990 Taurus."

"'90 Taurus, huh? Okay, tell me, when you drive faster, does the thumping increase its rate also?"

"Well, now that you mention it, I believe it does."

"Okay," he says. "And do you hear the sound when the car is cold, just after you start it in the morning, as well as when it's hot?"

"Actually," you say, "I don't think it does happen when the engine's cold."

"Okay," he says, "Leave the car here and pick it up at 5 p.m."

Which one of the two mechanics do you leave your car with? Silly question. Everyone I know says they'd leave it with the second mechanic. Why? Because he obviously knows what he's doing. And what made you think that he knows what he's doing?

His questions! We understand that it takes greater competence to ask good questions about a situation than it does to make pithy statements.

If you want your customers to respect your competence, ask good questions.

Here's a process to help you put this principle into practice. Let's call it the perception of competence process.

1. Consider each of your products or services.

2. Focusing on each one, identify the details of your customers' situations that would make them want your offerings.

3. Brainstorm a set of questions that would reveal those details.

4. Rewrite and edit those questions to reveal your understanding of the customers' experiences, objectives, problems, and feelings.

5. Use those questions.

Let's think through an example.

Step 1. Consider each of your products or services. My company sells a number of products and services. For purposes of this example, let's focus on one that every reader of this book will appreciate: customized sales training.

Step 2. Focusing on each one, identify the details of your customers' situations that would make them want your offerings. A company interested in customized sales training would:

- Have a sufficient quantity of outside salespeople, probably a minimum of fifteen or so.

- Be interested in improving the productivity or performance of those people.

- Believe that the salespeople could learn something from a training program.

- Probably have invested in packaged programs or public seminars in the past, and now are looking for a more individualized approach.

- Be willing and ready to pay for it.

Step 3. Brainstorm a set of questions that would reveal those details. We'll go into more detail on creating questions when we consider the third hat. We could create dozens if not hundreds of possibilities for each of the issues above, but for the purposes of this illustration, we'll focus on just one of those issues, "be interested in improving the productivity or performance of the salespeople." Let's assume that you've generated a set of questions that includes the following:

> *What makes you interested in customized sales training?*
>
> *How is your company doing relative to the competition?*
>
> *How is your company doing relative to its goals and objectives?*
>
> *What would improved sales performance mean to your company?*
>
> *What makes you think that your salespeople could improve?*

Having generated or brainstormed a series of questions, you're now ready to move to the next step in the process.

Step 4. Rewrite and edit those questions to reveal your understanding of the customer's experiences, objectives, problems, and feelings. The questions are designed to create in your customer the perception that you understand the situation. The situation consists of your customer's experiences, objectives, problems, and feelings. Let's take one of our first set of questions and work with it to create these kinds of perceptions.

Let's begin with, "What would improved sales performance mean to your company?"

Suppose we turned that into...

"I imagine that you have some sales goals that are a bit of a stretch for you, right?"

"What sort of experience have you had with sales training in the past?"

"Most companies who are talking to us about improved sales performance have come to the conclusion that either they don't have the resources to do it themselves, or it would be too costly in terms of time and money to attempt it. Would either of those circumstances describe your situation?"

"I'll bet you're frustrated with some of the things you see your salespeople doing, aren't you?"

Now, you may want to take exception to some of the language in these questions. However, the overall perception the questions create in your customers is that you understand their situation. In other words, you know what you're doing. In other words, you must be a competent salesperson. In other words, it's less risky dealing with you than with someone of less competence.

Step 5. Use those questions. It doesn't do any good to prepare them if you never discipline yourself to use them. Again, we'll discuss more details of using questions in Chapter 8. For now, I encourage you to begin using the questions you've created through this process.

If you do that, your customers will see you as competent. They'll be more inclined to deal with you and you'll gain a competitive edge, as well as greater competency at the second hat—becoming a Trusted Friend.

There's one more component of this hat to discuss: influencing your customers to trust you.

Gaining Your Customer's Trust

In my first professional sales position, I discovered that honesty and integrity were not just moral imperatives; they were highly prized qualities that prospects and customers valued. That meant ethics and integrity were also good business.

Everyone would rather work with honest, trustworthy people than with people who are dishonest and untrustworthy. Wouldn't you? If you're going to be someone your customers want to work with, you need to adhere rigorously to a consistent set of ethics and that brings us to the next principle.

⚓ *People trust people who have integrity.*

A good starting point is focusing on integrity. Webster's defines integrity as: "intactness, firmness of character." Firmness of character is the overarching quality that transcends everything you do, if you want to earn your customer's trust. It gives shape and substance to the more specific list of ethical commandments that follows. Firmness of character, translated into your sales behavior, means that you do what you say you're going to do and you are what you portray yourself to be. In other words, your customers and your colleagues can count on you to act honestly and consistently. They trust you. The salespeople who earn their customers' trust by being people of character and people of integrity have an immeasurable edge over the competition.

Not long ago, I was financing a new marketing project by selling limited partnership investments. I decided to offer the investments to the people who knew me best and who were acquainted with my work: my clients. I organized a number of small investor information meetings with groups of my clients. At one of the meetings, during the informal question and answer session that followed my presentation, one of my clients announced that, regardless of the details of the investment, he knew me to be a man of integrity, and that was good enough for him. Another chimed right in and agreed, saying he had confidence in my integrity also.

I was touched. I told them both that their saying that was one of the highest compliments they could pay me. Their trust in my integrity made doing business together much easier.

Integrity—being a person of solid, reliable character—is the overarching concept for all the specific ethical guidelines that follow. It's a quality of character that emanates from you like light reflected from a diamond. In fact, a diamond is a great visual image to convey the concept of integrity (see Figure 6-1).

FIGURE 6-1

A diamond is one of the hardest substances known. It's almost impossible to make a dent in one. For hundreds and thousands of years, a diamond can remain the same. That's like integrity; it doesn't change, but remains solid and not subject to the temptations that swirl around it.

A diamond purely reflects any light that shines on it. A salesperson with integrity makes everyone look good—customers, bosses, support staff, and associates.

A diamond is of great value, and so is integrity. As a sales consultant, I'm often asked what one should look for when contemplating hiring a salesperson. My reply is always the same. More than skill or knowledge, you should look for qualities of character. There is no quality of character more valuable to a salesperson than integrity. It's the first quality to look for when you're hiring salespeople.

One of the services I provide for my clients is to interview prospective salespeople, offering my client a second opinion as to the suitability of the individuals for the job. In one case I interviewed a candidate for a position as a mortgage originator. In the course of the conversation, the candidate confided in me that, since he had recently moved to west Michigan from a much larger metropolitan area, he discovered that pay scales were lower here than where he came from. So he changed his salary history on his resume and application form, stating that he had made less than he really did. His reasoning was that a potential employer in west Michigan would never be able to pay him that much, and he wouldn't get the job.

I could certainly understand his reasoning. The only problem was that his actions revealed a lack of integrity. He lied on the resume, he lied on the application, and he lied to my client in the interview process. Regardless of how well-meaning and reasonable the lie was, it was still a lie. I immediately decided to recommend that he not be hired. A person who would lie on a resume would lie to the boss and would lie to the customers.

I'm going to vary from my general approach in that I'm not going to discuss processes for implementing this principle. There isn't any process for developing ethical behavior. Rather, there are rules. To be seen as a trustworthy person, follow these nine commandments.

Nine Commandments for Ethical Salespeople

1. **Don't intentionally misrepresent anything.** Never, never, never lie to a customer. About anything. Period.

2. **Fix any important misunderstandings that you can.** It's possible that your customers will form incorrect ideas about some of the products you represent or the services that come with them. It's also possible that they will misunderstand things about your competitors, or about the needs and statements of other people who work in their organizations.

It's very tempting, when these misunderstandings work in your favor, to ignore them. However, that's not dealing with integrity. When you become aware of any significant misunderstanding your customer has that impacts the buying decision or the larger relationship, you need to correct it. This doesn't mean that you need to set customers straight on their political beliefs or their views on the controversial call in Sunday's football game. It does mean that, on the important issues that affect the sale, allowing misunderstandings to exist is an act of passive dishonesty on your part. Correct them when you can.

3. **Work hard for your employer.** It's easy for a salesperson to give in to the temptation to cut corners when it comes to working a full day, every day. After all, who really knows if you hit your first call at 9 a.m. instead of 8:30 a.m.? Who knows if you take a 30-minute coffee break between calls? Who knows if you make it home by 3 p.m. some days, and take a number of afternoons off to visit the golf course or the swim club during the summer? All these are examples of shortchanging your employer in ways that, in all probability, no one will ever know about except you.

   That's my point. *You* will know. A code of ethics is easy to live by when everyone is watching. It's a real test of character when your ethics are tested in situations when no one else knows, and you know you can get away with something.

   You owe your employer consistent, full days of your best efforts. Delivering anything less is unethical.

4. **If ethics are at stake, always be willing to trade a short-term loss for the sake of a long-term gain.** This is another definition of integrity—the courage and conviction to walk away from an unethical short-term gain in return for a long-term gain. In other words, always be willing to give up a sale or some immediate advantage if you must stretch the truth or act unethically to get it.

   For example, you may have an opportunity to acquire a quick sale because your customer has misunderstood the specifications or features of your product. It's tempting to take the order and not say anything, but that would not be ethical. The ethical salesperson will correct the customer and lose the immediate gain that the sale would have brought. The payoff, however, is the long-term gain in your reputation for integrity. A long-term gain achieved ethically is always worth more than *any* short-term advantage.

5. **Do what you say you are going to do.** This isn't as simple as it sounds. One of the obvious implications of doing what you say you're going to do is that you must not say you are going to do something that you know you can't do. In other words, don't overpromise. That's difficult to do when you're in the middle of a competitive situation over a nice piece of business, and you know the competition is overpromising to get the sale. But if you're going to be an ethical salesperson, you won't overpromise because you know you won't be able to do what you say you're going to do.

   There's another implication to this rule: You must be organized enough to follow through on your promises. The most honest person in the world can be perceived as unreliable if not organized enough to follow through on promises made. If you say you're going to call a customer back on Thursday, make sure that you have a tickler file, day-planner, computer program, or some other system that will remind you to call back when Thursday comes. That's being ethical.

6. **Give liberally.** As a professional salesperson, you enjoy a challenging job with a lot of freedom and a substantial income level. The world is full of people who would love to have that. You're one of life's more fortunate people.

   I think that means that you have a greater than average responsibility to give back to society. Give freely of your money to charitable or religious causes, and give liberally of your time and expertise to the organizations that you can help. Your expertise, your time, your people skills, your organizational skills, your confidence, and your ability to get things done—all these are assets you can bring to the Boy Scouts, your church, the PTA, and a thousand other organizations that can use your abilities.

   Because you are more blessed with talent, time, and money than most of the population, you have a greater responsibility to use them all for purposes other than just your own edification. Nido Qubein said, "Service to others is the rent you pay for taking up space on this earth. The richer the space, the higher the rent." Give liberally.

7. **Recognize those who help you.** It's easy to get into the mind-set that you alone are responsible for your success. After all, you're out there all alone, fighting the battle every day. Nobody else knows what good work you did in getting that account, or how hard it is some days when nothing goes your way.

   In spite of this, you couldn't do your job without the support of a whole group of people back at the office. Your manager gave you an opportunity and nurtured you along. The inside people have cleaned up more than a few of your messes, and they have positively impressed many of your customers. Others have put lots of time and energy into creating the products that ultimately provide your livelihood.

   All of these people, and probably dozens of others, have contributed in significant ways to your success. It is just as dishonest to fail to recognize them as it is to misrepresent a product. Ethical salespeople recognize the people who have helped them.

8. **Never give up.** This may seem an odd rule in a section on ethics, but I believe that giving up is the same as going home early or taking extra days off without anybody's approval. Both shortchange yourself as well as your employer.

   When you give up prematurely on a sale, or you give up on yourself and give in to negative thinking, you're choosing to deprive yourself and your employer of the full benefit of your talent and time. That's unethical.

9. **Don't speak badly about anyone.** In my first sales position, when I was selling amplification equipment, there were twenty-nine major installations purchased in my territory. I got the order for twenty-eight of those deals. My stomach still gets a little tight whenever I remember one of my crucial sales calls to the twenty-ninth customer.

   During the course of the conversation, she stopped me and said, "You know, I really don't like it that you're so negative about your competitor." I was stunned, embarrassed, and flustered. I turned beet red and blurted out an apology. But that was the end of that deal.

   I lost the deal because I had spoken badly about my competitor. That was an intensely painful lesson for me. I resolved never to make that mistake again.

As I matured, I realized that, when you negatively judge any-one, you really say more about yourself than you do about the other person. Speaking badly about a competitor, your boss, your company, or another customer always makes you look bad. Beside that, it's unethical.

Trying on the Second Hat

So I have you convinced and a little overwhelmed. How do you take these principles and processes and make them a part of your every-day routine? Here are the principles we considered:

1. *People find reasons to buy from people they are comfortable with, who they trust and respect.*
2. *Relationships save the customer time and mitigate the risk.*
3. *People are most comfortable with people who are like themselves.*
4. *People perceive you as competent not so much by what you say, but rather by what you ask.*
5. *People trust people who have integrity.*

We articulated the processes that will help you unleash the power of those principles. They include:

- The reflective process and
- The perception of competency process.

Then, of course, there were the Nine Commandments for Ethical Salespeople.

Where to start? Make a hard and fast, absolute decision, a decision that you will never reconsider. The decision is that you will deal with integrity in every situation. Period. No questions, no limitations, no exceptions. Once you've made that decision, you won't have to wrestle with every decision and every temptation. You will already have made the decision once and for all. Believe me, it's a whole lot easier and less stressful in the long run to make that decision and then never to quibble over it again, than it is to give yourself lots of room for maneuvering. When you do the latter, you struggle over every decision.

So begin with integrity. You'll find that decision will have an impact on your routine and your relationships almost daily.

Now that you know where you stand, you can begin to focus on your customer in a more sensitive fashion. Take one of the three areas for reflective behavior—communication style, language, or connections—and begin to play with it. Decide to focus on that one area for a month or two, and see how much sharper you can become at both assessing and reflecting. When you feel that you're doing it naturally, without having to think about it, move on to another area.

The competency questions will require more structured work. You might want to talk with your manager about them. This really is a great project for a group of you and your colleagues to work on together. Suggest that under your manager's guidance, the group could develop a set of competency questions that everyone could use. Then, plug away at it, one product or service at a time.

If that approach doesn't appeal to you, then pick one product to focus on and spend a couple of weeks working on the competency questions for that product. As you experiment with them, you'll find it easier and easier to create similar questions for the other products or services you represent.

That will get you off to a great start in making this hat fit.

Wearing the Second Hat

When you've fully incorporated these competencies, you'll find your confidence level skyrocketing and your sales paralleling that trajectory. Here's what you'll be doing:

You'll be able to meet and interact with any person confidently, of no matter what personality or background, because you'll be reflecting the other person's styles, language, and connections in a professional, disciplined fashion. Not only that, but you'll be getting most of the deals when there appears to be little difference between your offering and your competitor's. Your relationships will be the tiebreakers.

You'll feel better about yourself because you'll recognize that you are becoming perceived as a person of integrity. You'll enjoy the growing reputation of someone who is competent and trustworthy. Your customers will refer you to others and look for reasons to do business with you.

You will have become a Trusted Friend.

APPLICATION: USING THE SIX HATS TO TURN CHALLENGES INTO OPPORTUNITIES

Challenge: Voice Mail is driving me crazy!
It seems that I can never get through
to the people I want to talk to.

Welcome to the club. Not so many years ago, there was no such thing as voice mail. Today, it is almost impossible to call a customer on the phone and get directly to the person. The electronic gatekeeper, voice mail, stands in the way. Voice mail has become the number one irritant for salespeople in the Information Age.

There's a good reason for that. If you can't communicate with your customers, you can't get to see them. If you can't get to see them, you've been knocked out of the sales process. Unless you learn to work electronically, the likelihood of your making a sale is dramatically reduced.

Voice mail is one of those irritating issues that threaten the very heart of what you do. You've got to solve the voice mail dilemma or you won't be in business very long.

APPLYING THE SIX HATS

Let's begin by putting on the first hat, Astute Planner. Recognize that being connected to voice mail is one of the most likely outcomes of your telephone call. Don't be surprised when you call a customer and are routed to voice mail. Instead, be prepared. Imagine that you are given the ability to create a 30-second radio commercial and beam it directly to your customer. What would be in that commercial?

That's the attitude to take. Before you make each telephone call, prepare a 30-second radio commercial (your voice mail message). Then you're prepared for the likely occurrence of being routed to a voice mail system.

Next, put on the third hat, Skillful Influencer. You must put as much skill into your voice mail message as possible, influencing the customer to take action. It's important to focus on the action that you want the customer to take. If you're cold-calling for a first appointment, the action you want the customer to take is to get back to you, either in person or via E-mail or fax. If you're following up on a proposal or a previous visit, you want a different action from the customer. Keep clearly in mind the action you want the customer to take, and bring all your skills of influencing, using the presentation process as best you can, to deliver a powerful message. Don't sell your product; sell a return call. Give them a reason to call you back.

The presentation, like any other, should traverse through the steps of the presentation process. Identify a need or interest you believe your customer has, identify something you can do to assist with that need, list the benefits, and ask for action. Use your language and tone of voice to convey competence and confidence and to make your customer comfortable with you. It's the influencing presentation process capsulized in 30 seconds.

As long as you have your Skillful Influencer hat on, you can use it to take a broader view of the situation and create a series of communications, of which your voice mail message is merely one piece. As you know, the object of your efforts is to influence the customer to take action. In this case, the action is to call you back or to make an appointment to see you. Think about using alternate media to make a series of contacts with customers, to precondition them to respond to your call. For example, you might send a letter, follow it with an E-mail message, follow that with a fax, and then make your phone call.

A few years ago one of my clients, an advertising agency, developed an incredibly creative way to precondition the customer to accept the initial phone call. Here's how the program worked. They first qualified a list of 100 people they wanted to see. During the first week of the program, they sent each of the 100 a small box, wrapped in plain brown paper, with a hand-printed mailing address on it and no return address. In the box was a sugar cube with a small printed message saying, "Keep it sweet." Nothing else. You can imagine the curiosity aroused in the people receiving that box.

The second week, another package came in the mail. It was wrapped and addressed in the same way, only this time, the box contained a lemon. The message read, "Don't let it go sour."

Week three came and a third box arrived. Same wrapping, same appearance. This package contained some tinsel foil with the message, "Make it sparkle." Week four arrived, and the anticipated delivery of the fourth box. In it was the business card of the salesperson with a note that said, "I'll be calling you for an appointment." You may be interested in the result. One hundred percent of the recipients of that series of packages made appointments with the sales reps. The negative effect of voice mail was overcome by creatively preconditioning the customers to respond to your call.

There are frequent occasions when you encounter voice mail and you're well down the road of the sales process. It's not your first call; it's a subsequent visit with a customer you know. If you find yourself in this situation, apply all the strategies and tactics of the Skillful Infuencer.

However, the best strategy is to apply the hat of Adept Human Resources Manager, focusing on time management issues. Think ahead and avoid voice mail altogether. When you're with the customer, instead of agreeing to call and make an appointment for the next meeting, make the appointment right then. Explain that doing so, even if it is tentative and several months in the future, will save you both a phone call or two, and that means less time and less hassle for both of you. When you make the appointment, you've eliminated the need for a phone call and the frustration of voice mail.

Even if the situation or one of your schedules change, you can then use voice mail to your advantage by calling with a schedule change, leaving that message, and getting your customer's acknowledgment on *your* voice mail!

THE THIRD HAT:
EFFECTIVE CONSULTANT

What does it mean to be a consultant? Some people say a consultant is someone who borrows your watch, tells you what time it is, and then charges you for the information. As a consultant myself, I'd prefer a more positive definition: A consultant is someone you pay to help you understand your situation, and then to help you overcome problems and achieve objectives.

Notice first that there is a price. You must think highly enough of the consultant's capabilities to pay for them. People who work for free are generally worth exactly what you paid them.

One major thing you should expect of consultants, whether personal therapists, business consultants, financial consultants, management consultants, or sales consultants, is that they take the time to understand you and your situation. How can they provide you with any direction or assistance unless they understand who you are and what issues you're struggling with?

You should also expect consultants to help you with your problems and your objectives. Notice that there is both a positive and negative here. Sometimes you'll employ a consultant to help you with your problems; at other times your investment is even more valuable when the consultant helps you achieve your objectives.

What does all this have to do with selling in general and with the Six-Hat Salesperson specifically? Only this: In the Information Age, more and more of your customers want you to be a consultant to them. Put yourself in their shoes. Growing complexity, increasing competition, and time constraints all conspire to put pressure on them. Many of your customers have too much to do and not enough time in which to do it. So they instinctively look for someone who can take some of the burden off them—someone who understands their situation and helps them solve their problems and achieve their objectives. Customers may not admit it or even be aware of it, but that instinct to delegate or download is a real part of every decision to hire a consultant.

You can be that consultant to many of your customers. You can understand them better than anyone else, and then use that deeper and more detailed understanding to help them solve their problems and achieve their objectives. You're paid not in hourly billable time, but in sales commissions.

Becoming a consultant to your customers is not just an effective competency because of your customers' situations. If you only look at the competency from the salesperson's perspective, it is still an incredibly effective competency. That's because the largest, most important part of the sales process is accomplished when you understand the customer.

There was a time, in the product-focused days gone by, when understanding the customer was less important than understanding your product. Those days were squeezed into oblivion by the proliferation of "me-too" products. In a world where products and services are more and more alike, the power has moved from the product to the customer. In the Information Age, 75 percent of your success in making the sale lies in understanding the customer.

Apply the principles and practices of the second hat, Effective Consultant, and your sales performance will take a quantum leap forward. No matter what you're selling, you can take on the role of consultant to achieve Information Age success for you and your company.

Here's an example of how this idea of being a consultant to your customer can be applied even in a very simple selling situation.

Suppose you work in a retail store, selling women's dresses. A customer walks in and begins examining a rack of evening dresses. You could approach her and say something like, "We've got some new designer dresses on this rack in the back." That would be an example of a traditional, product-centered approach. You're focused on the products—the designer dresses—and don't take the time to understand the person.

On the other hand, you could take the consultant approach. You could say something like, "Are you just looking for a nice dress, or do you have a specific occasion in mind?"

You customer replies, "I've got a fancy company banquet to go to."

"Oh," you reply with a smile, " and what kind of impression do you want to make?"

Your customer smiles at you, "Something a little more eye-catching and a bit richer then everyone else."

"I imagine you'd look good in red," you say. "What other colors do you wear well?"

"Deep colors," she says. "You know, dark green, navy, black."

"I think I might have just the thing for you. Come back here and let me show you these new designer dresses."

Which of the two approaches do you think will provide the best results? Silly question. When you take the extra moment or two and spend the extra bit of energy to understand your customers first, and then assist them with their problems and objectives, you'll find them to be much more receptive.

If you can apply the consultant hat in this simple, brief selling encounter, think of the potential in longer, more complex selling situations.

The third hat, Effective Consultant, can be one of your most powerful competencies. Let's examine the first principle:

⚓ *Your customers want to be understood.*

There is something in human beings that hungers to be understood. This is especially true when we're considering a high-risk decision. Sometimes the hunger is almost visceral, deep down beneath our consciousness. At other times we're very aware of our desire to be understood. Regardless, the desire is always there.

I'm reminded of Steven Covey's great challenge, from *The Seven Habits of Highly Effective People:* "Seek first to understand, and then to be understood." What a great expression of this hat and this first principle.

In the past few months, my wife and I have been considering remodeling our house. We've called four companies, all referrals or recommendations to us. Salespeople from two of the four actually showed up. The salesperson from the first company looked at our sketches, listened to us for a few minutes, then got a window sample from his car and spent the next thirty minutes presenting that window to us.

We didn't buy. We were looking for a deck with French doors opening onto it, not new windows. This salesperson was obviously product-focused—a window salesperson, not a consultant.

The other salesperson spent almost an hour with us, asking about what we had in mind, suggesting ideas and getting our responses, and getting to know what we are really looking for.

He's due back in a week or so with a proposal. I don't think he'll bring a window sample with him. I do think he'll have a proposal that we'll seriously consider, and at this point, we are inclined to do business with him. Why? Because he took the time and invested the energy to understand us and our situation.

From our perspective as buyers, we're favorably impressed with salespeople who take the time to understand us. The same thing is true of your customers. As complexity and confusion grow in their business lives, they're more and more favorably impressed with salespeople who take the time to understand them.

It's a bit more complicated than that, however, from the point of view of the salesperson, and that brings us to the second principle:

⚓ Understanding your customer is like peeling an onion.

I know, that's one of the craziest things you've heard. Trust me for a minute as we consider this principle.

Suppose you've just come back from your company's annual sales meeting. For three days, you sat in meetings and ate hotel food. Now you're home and you'd like nothing more than a cold beer and a home-cooked meal. You suggest a big salad for dinner and your spouse agrees, suggesting that you peel the onion.

You take out a big, fat Bermuda onion, about the size of a softball. You position it carefully on a cutting board and root through the drawer until you find a sharp knife. Steadying the onion with one hand, you slice neatly through the center of the onion, splitting it evenly in two.

You pick up one of the onion halves and examine it from the inside. You note that it has layers and layers, each deeper and more tightly compressed than the one surrounding it. You begin to peel the onion, stripping off the skin. As you pull off the skin of the onion, you notice that the skin is thin, dry, and crinkly, with very little scent. However, as you peel each layer, one at a time, you soon come to the conclusion that each layer is more strongly scented than the one above it, and that the strength of the onion's pungency comes from the inside out.

That's the best way to understand this principle. Just as there are layers and layers to an onion, so there are layers and layers to your customer. Just as the superficial layers of an onion are thin and mild, the superficial levels of your customers have little strength. But as you peel the onion deeper and deeper, the strength increases. So too with your customer.

FIGURE 7-1

Peeling the Onion

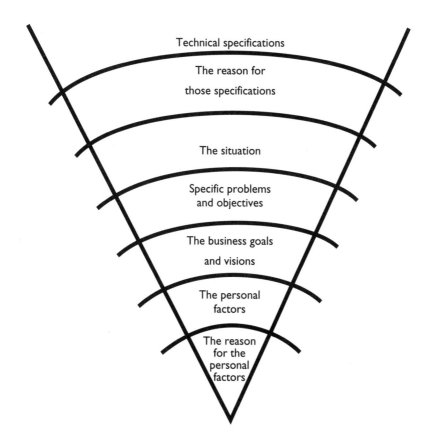

Let's apply this specifically to understanding your customer in a sales situation. Look at Figure 7-1. Imagine that it's a slice of that onion. On the very surface are the technical specifications for the product or service the customer wants. For example, let's say you call on one of your customers who says, "I need to purchase three green metal widgets that are one-half inch by 6 inches." Many salespeople would respond, "Okay, they are $2.50 each." In this example, the salesperson understood the customer at the most superficial level—technical specifications—and responded in kind.

But you can go deeper in understanding the customer by discovering the reason behind these specifications.

Our rep, when confronted with the same request, might say, "What are you going to use them for?" or, "Is there a reason you asked for metal instead of plastic?" This kind of response will uncover the next level, the *reason* for the specifications.

There's more. The *situation* refers to the history behind the need and the circumstances surrounding the need. For example, let's say that our salesperson now replies, "What's your situation? Why is this an issue now?" The customer's reply to that question uncovers a deeper layer of need.

You're still pretty close to the surface. When you uncover the specific problems and objectives that underlie the original request, you've gone deeper in your understanding of the customer. Returning to our example, suppose your customer says, "We're having a problem with our second shift's production. The line keeps breaking down. Our maintenance supervisor wants to stockpile some of the parts that have needed regular replacing."

Now you have an understanding of the specific problems and objectives. But there is more: Suppose you ask how that problem affects the rest of the company. Suppose that in reply your customer explains the effect of the breakdown on production, net profits, and overtime pay for the second shift. Now you understand the customer at yet a deeper level.

But you can go deeper still. When you ask how those systemic problems affect your customer's business goals and you learn that it's particularly troublesome because your customer's goals are to increase net profits by 5 percent this year, you understand the customer at an even deeper level.

You take a significant plunge deeper when you are able to understand how the situation affects the individual with whom you're talking. For example, when you know someone well enough to ask, "How can I make you look good in this transaction?" and get an honest response, you've penetrated to a new layer of understanding.

Finally, when you understand the individual motivations—the reasons for the personal factors—you understand the customer at levels that few salespeople ever approach. That's the level the masters work at. Those motivations are often emotionally driven. When you understand the customer's emotions—how the situation makes him or her feel—you've arrived at the heart of the onion.

The Six-Hat salesperson understands the similarity between peeling an onion and understanding your customer. Bring the two principles together and the results can be amazingly powerful.

Here are two easy-to-remember acronyms to help you work with these principles: SPOO and PIE. SPOO stands for the customer's *specific problems or objectives*. In order to peel the onion and understand your customer, you must get to this level by uncovering these two issues.

Most salespeople consider themselves to be problem solvers. They find an opportunity to sell their products or services when their customers have problems to solve. That's fine, as far as it goes. But just as important as helping your customers solve their problems is helping your customers achieve their objectives. Focusing on understanding your customer's objectives opens up at least as many opportunities for you to sell your products and services, and forces you to understand what is important to your customers.

For example, suppose you're selling production equipment. If your customer doesn't have any problems with the current state of the production line, you may think you have no opportunities to sell your products. But if you were to peel the onion and discuss objectives with your customer, you might find that that company wants to have a 15 percent increase in capacity over the next twelve months. That's an objective, not a problem, and it's a great opportunity for you. Until you understand both sides of the picture, the customer's specific problems or objectives, you can't really function as a consultant to your customers. Remember SPOO.

Then remember PIE. Not apple pie, but rather a simplified illustration of the onion. Here's an easy-to-remember and easy-to-use version. Note that Figure 7-2 simplifies the original onion to three levels. The most superficial are *problems or objectives*. The second layer consists of the *implications*. In other words, you take the time to understand the consequences of successfully solving the problem or meeting the objective, as well as the consequences of not doing so. You probe those consequences or implications for the company as well as for the individuals with whom you are working. For example, you may have discovered a customer wants to increase production capacity by 15 percent. When you enter into a discussion with that company that causes you to understand the consequences to the company of not increasing capacity, and the ramifications of doing so, that's good. When you understand what

FIGURE 7-2

The Customer's Pie

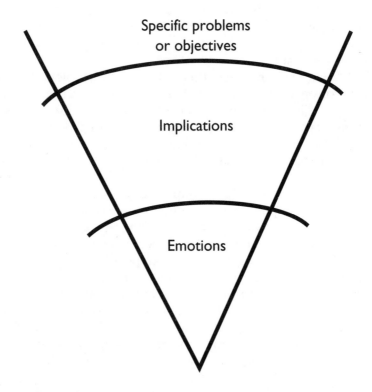

those consequences are for the individuals within the company, you've just peeled the onion a little deeper.

For example, your customer might say, "If we don't get the 15 percent increase in capacity, we'll not be able to handle the new contract from Ford. If we can't handle the new contract, they could very well take our current business away from us, because they want to consolidate vendors. That's a major portion of our business. If that goes, we'd have a difficult time surviving." Now that you know the consequences for the company, you've discovered the *implications* level of the onion.

Peeling further may result in your individual customer sharing the personal implications: "I might not have a job."

Now, let's peel the onion one more level deeper and discover the *emotional* level. How do the implications make the individuals within that company feel? When your customer confides in you that he or she would feel "really proud" to have helped achieve that increase, and "scared about what might happen" if the increase is not achieved, you will have peeled the onion in a very significant, powerful way. You now understand the customer probably better than any of your competitors, because you've focused on understanding the customer's *SPOO* and *PIE*.

As always, the question is, "How do you implement these principles?" The answer is by mastering the single most powerful sales tool available to Six-Hat Salespeople.

┬ *The question is the key.*

A good sales question is the single most effective tool you can use to bring you the knowledge you need. Stringing together a series of well-designed questions can be your most effective strategy to gain an edge in this most critical part of the sales process. There is simply nothing you can do in a face-to-face interchange with your customer that is more powerful then asking a Good Sales Question (hereafter referred to as a GSQ, see Figure 7-3). Your knowledge of the customer, the depth and nature of your relationship with your customer, his or her perception of your competence, the level of trust developed between your customer and yourself—all of these are impacted by your ability to create and use GSQs. If you're going to wear the consultant's hat, you *must* master the competency of asking good sales questions.

FIGURE 7-3

The Question is the Key

A GSQ is the primary means of knowing your customer and collecting information. It also does much more for a Six-Hat Salesperson than that. A GSQ functions in several other positive ways.

First, a well-phrased, appropriately timed question *directs your customer's thinking*. It's almost impossible to be asked a question and not think of the answer. I'm not sure whether it's something in our basic humanity or whether we're conditioned since birth to always think of the answer to a question. To illustrate, I'll ask you a question, but I want you to *not* think of the answer. Here's the question: "How old are you?"

If you're like most of us, you thought of the answer, even after I indicated you shouldn't. That's the point! There is something in all of us that makes us think of the answer when we're asked a question. To not do so takes a steel will and great discipline.

Now, consider where the decision to buy your products or services takes place. Doesn't it happen in the mind of your customer? The way you penetrate that mind and get it working in your direction is to ask GSQs. Questions shape the direction in which your customer's mind works.

Here's an illustration. Suppose you're shopping for a new car. The salesperson asks you, "Which is more important to you, good fuel economy or quick pickup?" Until asked, you hadn't really thought of it that way. The salesperson's question helps you understand what you really think, and directs your mind along a certain course. So it is with your customers. You can use GSQs to shape and steer the direction of your customers' thinking.

Second, a question is a powerful tool to *build relationships* with your customers. Have you ever struck up a conversation with someone in a social setting and discovered that person was very interested in you? He or she asked about what you did for a living, and showed interest in your hobbies, your family, or your opinions. You left the conversation thinking, "What a nice person!"

What made you like that person? It was the way he or she was interested in you. And how did you know he or she was interested in you? By the questions asked.

The law of reciprocity states that people will respond to you in the way in which you first act toward them. That's Dale Carnegie 101. Show interest in your customer, and your customer will reciprocate by showing interest in you.

The way you show interest in someone is to ask them questions about themselves. You can ask personal questions even if you know the answer. The purpose of the question is not necessarily to get the answer, it's to build a relationship.

In Chapter 5 we discussed another powerful function of a good question. A series of GSQs *creates the perception of your compe-*

tence. In other words, your prospect sees you as competent and trustworthy not necessarily by what you **say,** but rather by what you **ask.**

There is yet one more function of a good question. This is the one you've been thinking about all along. A good question is your best means of *collecting the information* that will help you construct a sale by understanding the customer and the customer's situation. How do you know what a prospect thinks or what the situation is, unless you ask a question? The question helps you to see what's in the mind and heart of your prospect.

The Six-Hat Salesperson knows that a sale is created only after the salesperson thoroughly understands the customer. Often, in a competitive situation, the salesperson who best knows the customer gains the advantage. The way to acquire that knowledge of the customer is to use GSQs skillfully.

Opening the Sale

One of the best applications for well-constructed, appropriately timed questions is early in the sales process when you're attempting to peel the onion and uncover the customer's SPOO and PIE.

Remember, the sale often goes not to the person with the best product or price, but to the one who does the best job of understanding the customer. Here's a real-life illustration.

I was asked by one of my clients to work with his sales force. The salespeople were having trouble closing sales. Let me describe what happened in a sales call I made with one of the salespeople.

We were selling HVAC equipment and the salesperson had an appointment with the prospect. We met the prospect and he explained that the building had been added onto several years before, but that nothing had been done to expand the capacity of the air conditioning unit. The company now wanted to do something about that.

The salesperson asked to see the area in question. He measured the square footage of the room, taking detailed notes on a form attached to his clipboard. Then he asked to see the existing equipment. We went up into the attic where the equipment was located and the salesperson studied the existing unit, estimating the distance from the equipment to the addition.

He ended his information collecting by saying to the prospect, "I'll fax you a proposal in a couple days. Will that be okay?" The prospect said yes.

At this point, the salesperson had done an adequate job of understanding the technical specifications of the situation, but hadn't even begun to probe into some of the other aspects of the sale. I intervened and asked the following questions.

"If you like our proposal, what's the possibility that you'll buy it within the next few weeks?"

Here's what the prospect said: "Oh, none at all. I'm just collecting information for budgeting purposes. We won't actually buy anything until after the new fiscal year starts in January."

My salesperson didn't know that because he never asked. Instead, he proceeded on the erroneous assumption that the prospect was in a buying mode.

Next I asked about the situation. I said, "When we met, you said that the addition had been completed a few years ago, but that nothing had been done to upgrade the air conditioning. Tell me, what's changed about your situation? Why is this an issue now?"

He said, "Well, we added space to this building several years ago. It's always been stuffy in the new addition, but we got along okay. At least until last week, when we had a heat wave. The air conditioning system had to work so hard that it froze up. So we unplugged it to let the ice thaw. As the ice thawed, it dripped through the acoustical ceiling directly onto the president's desk. That's why we've decided to do something about it now!"

Then I said, "What are you looking for in a proposal?"

He said, "Just a ballpark figure we can use for budgeting purposes."

I turned to my salesperson and asked, "What's a rough estimate of what it'll take?"

He responded, "About $3,500."

Then I asked the prospect, "What can we do to make you look good in this process?"

He said, "I just want to get this off my desk. It's an extra project I don't need right now."

I said, "If we get you a ballpark figure and a set of literature you can show to the boss today, will that help?"

"That would be great," he said.

Finally I asked, "How will a decision be made?"

"Around here, the president makes those kinds of decisions. So I'll collect the information and give it to him, and he'll decide what to do from there."

"Could we see him?" I asked.

The prospect replied, "Would you?"

"We'd be happy to," I said. At that point, he made an appointment for us to talk to the president.

Let's analyze this experience. Without the use of GSQs, the salesperson would have wasted hours preparing and faxing the quote, and then wondering why he didn't close the sale. He was well-equipped to respond to the technical specifications, but he didn't have the faintest understanding of the customer's need and therefore had little chance of closing the sale. When we added the skillful use of GSQs, we uncovered the truth of the situation and positioned ourselves to capture the sale.

The question was the key.

That's how questions can be used to more completely understand the customer as you open the sale.

Questions can be used at every phase of the sales process, but they are particularly effective:

- In the initial probing meeting, to "open" the sale and understand the customer.
- During your presentation, to gather feedback from the customer.
- Following the presentation, to achieve agreement on a course of action.

The Processes

If you are going to become skilled at the use of GSQs, you need to master two processes:

1. Preparing questions word for word.
2. Using questions effectively.

PROCESS: PREPARING GOOD SALES QUESTIONS

When you're making a presentation, you don't always have to phrase everything you say perfectly. People will understand what you mean even if you're not totally accurate in your choice of words. It's acceptable to say "about 50 percent" instead of saying "49.27 percent."

However, that is not the case when you're phrasing questions. The language you use in your question must be perfect, because the words in your question direct your prospect's thinking. A little change in words can make a huge difference in your prospect's response.

I created a telemarketing program for one of my clients, and stopped in to see him a couple of months after the program was instituted. "How's it going?" I asked.

"Fine," he said "The telemarketers are creating lots of leads. But, I have a problem."

"What's your problem?" I asked.

"I can't get the salespeople to follow up on the leads," he replied. "So I have a question."

"What's the question?" I asked.

"How can I get the salespeople to follow up on the leads?"

I thought for a moment and replied, " I think that's the wrong question."

"What should I ask?"

"How can I get the leads followed up on?" I responded.

Let's consider what happened. When he asked, "How can I get the salespeople to follow up on the leads?" our thinking was directed to the salespeople. The solution to his problem would be limited to salespeople.

However, when we changed the question to "How can I get the leads followed up on?" we opened up a much larger range of possibilities. Maybe the telemarketers could follow up on them, maybe the owner or sales manager could, maybe the salespeople could, maybe some independent reps could. We opened the door to a world of possible solutions.

You see, a tiny change in wording in the phrasing of the question caused an enormous change in the direction of our thinking, and therefore a major shift in the solutions that followed. That's why it's important to phrase your key questions word for word—to make certain that they ask exactly what you want them to ask.

You'll be much more likely to phrase your questions accurately if you spend time preparing them first than if you attempt to do all your composing on the spur of the moment. That's not to say that you'll never create impromptu questions during the interaction with your customer. Of course you will. But you need to have your basic questions prepared before your meeting starts.

By taking the time to prepare questions first, you can be certain that they will be the most effective you can make them.

Step 1. Frame the situation. Begin by thinking about the situation you'll be encountering. Take a few moments to construct it in your mind. For example, suppose you will be meeting a new prospect for the first time. Imagine the setting, see the situation, and envision the person.

Then think about what you want to accomplish in that situation. In the example, you might have identified these objectives:

- Uncover the prospect's needs and interests.
- Qualify the prospect as a potential buyer.
- Attempt to set an appointment for a later date.
- Begin to create a trusting relationship with the prospect.

Now that you have both the situation and your objectives in mind, it's time to begin developing questions that will take you where you want to go.

Step 2. Brainstorm all the possibilities. Write down all the questions that you think you might ask. Don't worry about editing them at this point; just get as many questions down on paper as come into your mind. As you create your questions, keep the two basic types in mind: open-ended and closed-ended. An open-ended question is one that can't be answered in one word. It calls for an explanation, and there is no right or wrong answer. A closed-ended question is just the opposite; it calls for a specific bit of information. For example, "How do you feel about our proposal?" is an open-ended question, while "Who got the order?" is a closed-ended question. Each has a place in the hands of a Six-Hat Salesperson.

Step 3. Edit and refine. After you have created an exhaustive list of questions, go back over it and rewrite those that make the most sense to you. Judge each question by these three rules.

A. A good sales question doesn't intimidate the customer, imply blame, or cause anyone to lose face.

Consider the question, "What do you dislike about your current supplier?" That's a bad question. If the person you're speaking to is the one who selected that supplier, you're asking the person to admit a mistake. The question implies blame and causes the customer who answers it honestly to lose face. Rephrase the question to something like this: "What qualities or behaviors would you really like to see in a supplier?" That question will bring you the same information as the first one, but will do so in a positive, nonthreatening way.

B. A good sales question prompts the kind of thinking you want. Let's say you just presented your proposal. One of the questions you've thought about asking is, "Was there anything in the proposal we didn't address?" That question directs the customer to think about what is wrong with the proposal. Suppose you were to rephrase the question as, "How do you think this proposal will benefit you?" In that case, you've directed the customer to think about the positive aspects of the proposal. When you edit your list of questions, make sure they prompt the kind of thinking you want.

C. A good sales question asks for the level of information appropriate to the depth of the relationship. As you deepen your relationship with a customer, you can ask deeper questions. Some questions are totally inappropriate at the onset of a relationship, but perfectly appropriate when you've established some trust and comfort with your customer.

For example, you may want to ask your customer, "How well entrenched is the competition in your organization?" That question won't prompt an honest answer until you've created a deeper relationship with the customer.

That's why great salespeople are so good at building relationships. Their relationships allow them to know their customers more deeply, and that deeper knowledge enables them to present attractive solutions.

Step 4. Develop an effective sequence. Now that you've edited your questions and each question is as good as you can make it, sort them into the sequence you think will be most effective.

The sequence you use can be almost as important as the language of your questions. For example, you'll almost always want to start at the surface of the onion, asking questions about the most general and superficial subjects, and then gradually work your way into the heart of the onion with more pointed questions.

We'll discuss sequences in more detail in Chapter 8.

After you go through the process of creating good sales questions a few times, you'll find that you're using some questions over and over. Those good, comfortable questions can be in your toolbox as stock questions that you can use repetitively.

Some questions I've found to be particularly effective include:

- "Tell me about your business."
- "What's your situation?"
- "What would have to change for us to do more business with you?"

Step 5. Practice. Just one more little effort will add the icing to the cake and take you a long way toward becoming a master: Practice the questions once or twice. It'll only take a minute or two of your time. You'll be sure that the phrasing is comfortable for you, and the practice will help plant the questions in your mind.

With that, you're ready to use the single most powerful interpersonal tool in your tool box—a good sales question.

8

EFFECTIVE CONSULTANT: PART II

Using Questions Effectively

You've prepared your major questions word for word. Now it's time to master the process of actually using those questions to understand your customer more effectively. Here is the process:

1. Set the atmosphere.
2. Ask the questions effectively.
3. Listen constructively.
4. Respond positively.

Step 1. Set the atmosphere. Atmosphere refers to the emotional climate surrounding the interaction between you and your customer. Whether you acknowledge it or not, the customer "feels" something about you and about the time spent with you. The intensity of these feelings varies from person to person and situation to situation, but feelings are a part of every sales situation.

Does your customer feel comfortable with you? Are you honest and frank with one another? Is there an atmosphere of trust and respect? Does your customer feel that it's okay to be honest, detailed, and thorough in communicating with you?

If you could answer "yes" to all these questions, you'd describe the kind of emotional atmosphere you'd like to enjoy with your customers. Those questions describe the kind of emotional atmosphere that is most conducive to having your questions answered thoroughly and honestly.

Whose job is it to create a positive emotional atmosphere between you and your customer? It's yours. After all, you're the salesperson. You're the proactive agent who has a vested interest in achieving a positive outcome to this interaction. Because the outcome (the ultimate sale) is your responsibility, all of the means to that end, including the emotional atmosphere, are also your responsibility. In a world sprinkled with different kinds of customers—older, younger, male, female, pleasant, grumpy, quiet, or communicative—it is always your responsibility to fashion a positive emotional climate.

How do you create that kind of atmosphere? You apply the principle of reciprocity. This principle states that:

⚓ *Generally, people will respond to you in the way you first behave toward them.*

Reflect a moment and you'll realize that you know this to be true. As with many principles, salespeople don't always apply them in a disciplined and professional manner, even if they know them.

What happens when you meet someone who greets you with a really warm smile? Do you scowl back? Of course not; you smile back. The principle of reciprocity is at work.

Suppose you come home from a really bad day at work. Your car broke down, you were tossed out of a client's office and told never to come back, you lost a sale to your archcompetitor, and you stepped in a mud puddle halfway up to your knee. You come into your home, slam the door shut, throw your briefcase down, and kick the dog out of the way. Does your spouse then say to you, "Oh, honey, so nice to have you home"? I don't think so. In my experience, what generally happens is that my spouse acts toward me the way I first acted. I become the recipient of negative emotion—emotion that I initiated.

On and on it goes. If you want your customers to feel certain feelings when they deal with you, you need to create those feelings by first being what you want your customers to be. If you want your customers to be honest and thorough with you, you must first be honest and thorough with them. If you want them to be comfortable and trusting with you, you must first be comfortable and trusting with them. While it's important that you begin the interaction by modeling the emotion you want to create, it's not an isolated event that applies only to the first few minutes of an interaction. Rather you must be aware of your bearing and demeanor throughout every interaction you have with the customer.

Setting the atmosphere is a necessary first step in the process. Then, when you've begun to influence the emotional atmosphere surrounding the interaction, you're ready to ask your questions.

Step 2. Ask the questions effectively. Asking question effectively means using good sequences and delivering the questions properly. Let's look at sequences first.

Imagine a funnel with a large opening at the top and a small one at the bottom. That's an illustration for one type of questioning sequence. It graphically describes the amount of information your question is designed to elicit. The large opening at the top of the funnel indicates a great deal of information prompted by open-ended questions. The funnel narrows, indicating the continuously narrowing, more specific nature of your subsequent questions. You start with an open-ended question or two, and then slowly narrow the focus of the questions more and more precisely until you're asking very focused questions to collect specific information.

A good application of this technique is in a probing meeting when you are identifying the customer's needs and interests. Here's a specific sequence I call the 1-2-3 sequence: Start with *one* open-ended question. Then pick *two* topics out of the customer's response to probe more specifically, and ask *three* questions about each of the responses. Using this sequence of questions will almost always provide you with an opportunity to present a solution.

Here's an example. Suppose you're selling production equipment. You begin the funnel questioning sequence with an open-ended question. "John, tell me about the current state of your production line." John tells you that they've recently expanded to a second shift and that the line has been breaking down more frequently because of the increased wear and tear on the equipment. You decide to probe two areas—wear and tear on the equipment, and the implication that business is growing because they've gone to two shifts.

You decide to ask three more precise questions about each of those two areas. You say, "It sounds like your business is growing nicely," and pause to turn the statement into a question. John replies, "Yes, we've recently added a major new contract with one of our customers who is doing very well, and acquired three new customers from our representative in the next state."

You phrase your next question. "If things are going that well, are you thinking about investing in upgrading your equipment?" John replies, "Yes, there's talk about it, but we haven't decided what to do yet."

Now phrase the third question of this sequence. "It might help your decision-making process to have some information about the latest equipment. Should I spend some time with you and the engineer to show you what some of your options are?"

John replies, "That probably wouldn't be a bad idea."

You have just used the funnel sequence, specifically the 1-2-3 version, to identify an opportunity to present a piece of equipment. It's been my experience that the 1-2-3 sequence, in the hands of a skillful salesperson, almost always uncovers a potential opportunity.

OH?

One of the most powerful and useful GSQs is the interrogative, "Oh?" What happens when you ask someone the question, "Oh?" and then pause? Try it. When someone tells you something, say "Oh?" and then be quiet. The person has to jump in to explain, and in that explanation gives you more information and generally uncovers a deeper layer of truth.

"Oh" occupies a special place in the toolbox of the Six-Hat Salesperson. I believe you can use "Oh" three or four times during the course of a conversation without the other person even being aware of it. It's a small and inconspicuous word. As soon as you interject it, the other person starts thinking about what he or she is going to say in response to it. So "Oh" goes unnoticed as a question.

DEEPER LAYERS OF TRUTH

I've named one of the most powerful questioning sequences "deeper layers of truth." Using it effectively is one of the skills that can mark you as a truly outstanding sales performer. The sequence derives its power from the fact that most salespeople are content to interact with their prospects and customers at superficial levels. They never really take the time or the risk to penetrate deeper than the most superficial conversations. As a result, they're left with a cursory understanding of their prospects and shallow relationships with their customers.

Remember the onion graphic from Chapter 7? That analogy also provides a graphic illustration of the concept of deeper layers of truth. Imagine your prospects as onions. When you deal with them on the surface, you stay on the edge where it's not too pungent, nor too close to the heart of the matter.

While it's easy and safe to remain on the surface and interact with people on only the most superficial levels, it also keeps you away from the heart of the issue, where the decisions are really made. However, some salespeople—those who want to excel—develop the ability to penetrate below the surface, to reach the deeper layers of truth. Like cutting into the heart of the onion, they gain the ability to interact with the deeper issues and concerns of their prospects.

Let me illustrate. Suppose you visit a purchasing agent to whom you recently delivered a quote. In the course of the conversation you say something like, "How did we do on that proposal?"

She says, "Not bad, really."

You respond, "Great. When will we know what you're going to do?"

"We think we'll have it resolved soon," she says.

At this point most salespeople would leave, thinking that they have collected the most pertinent available information. In fact, they have engaged in a very superficial conversation. They have been held to the outer edge of the onion and haven't penetrated to deeper levels of truth.

Now, it may be true that the salesperson's quotation was not bad. It may also be true that the customer thinks they'll have it resolved soon. However, neither of those replies tells the salesperson anything of value. They don't provide any information on which to attempt to bring the sale to conclusion. The Six-Hat salesperson will not accept these superficial answers, but will instead direct the conversation to deeper levels.

The technique for doing so is incredibly simple. Just ask for further clarification and question your prospect's answer. Use questions like "Oh?" or "What do you mean by ...?" Let's see how this works.

In the sample conversation when your prospect says, "Not bad, really," you say, "Oh?" and pause to let her speak. The purchasing agent pauses for a moment and responds, "Yes, you were one of the lowest bids." Now, that's a bit more informative. It's just as true as the statement "Not bad," but it's more detailed, more revealing, and therefore true on a deeper level. But it's not deep enough, so you respond, "Does that mean you are seriously considering our proposal?"

"Yes."

Is low price the only factor on which the business will be awarded?"

"No. There are a number of other things we're considering."

"What are some of those?"

"Well, obviously, we're concerned about the reputation of the supplier, and the ability to meet our specifications and deadlines."

"And how do you feel about our proposal based on those issues?"

"We are a little concerned about your ability to meet our deadlines."

At this point, the salesperson has penetrated to deeper layers of truth and is talking with the prospect on a level that can make a real difference. In this instance, the conversation has developed almost to the point of negotiation. As the conversation continues, the salesperson will have excellent information on which to make some important decisions. The salesperson will understand exactly where the proposal stands and what has to be done to manage the sale to fruition.

Compare that to the salesperson who was content to accept the first, superficial reply. The second salesperson chose to dig for deeper layers of truth by asking "Oh?" and "Why?" questions and by asking for further or more precise clarification.

This tactic of digging for deeper layers of truth can be used successfully at several points in the sales process. For example, you can use it when you're probing to discover the prospect's deeper needs and higher-priority goals before presenting your product or service.

Suppose you are interviewing a prospect in your first meeting. In response to your question he says, "Yes, we are thinking about upgrading our computer network." Most salespeople would accept that superficially true answer and move on from there to something like, "Good. Can we make a proposal?"

The salesperson skilled at digging for deeper layers of truth will take the time to understand the prospect more completely and precisely. By doing so, you acquire a deeper knowledge of the prospect and, therefore, an edge over the competition. Some questions you could ask in this situation might include these:

"Why are you considering that?"

"What do you hope to gain by the upgrade?"

"What problems are you trying to solve?"

"When exactly do you expect to begin and finish this project?"

"Do you have a budget figure in mind?"

Only after digging for deeper layers of truth does the Six-Hat Salesperson move on to the next step in the process. At that point, you have far better information than the average salesperson, and are much better equipped to manage the sale to its successful completion.

Digging for deeper layers of truth carries the additional fringe benefit of causing your prospect to perceive you as competent and professional. As you take the time to intelligently probe the issue, you reveal yourself as a knowledgeable, professional person. The prospect forms an opinion of you based not on what you say, but on what you ask. Also, by understanding the prospect more completely and deeply, you become equipped to present a proposal that will more precisely address the prospect's deeper concerns.

Here are some of the stages in the sales process at which the deeper layers of truth tactic is most effective:

- When you are probing for needs and priorities.
- When you are presenting and demonstrating, to understand a prospect's reactions.
- When you are closing, to uncover deeper concerns and objections.
- When you are attempting to understand the personal as opposed to the business side of a prospect.

Uncovering deeper layers of truth isn't easy. It requires that a salesperson gain skills in asking questions and have the courage to hang in there when the natural reaction is to leave.

Funneling and deeper layers of truth are both questioning sequences that have broad application. You can use them to move your Six-Hat sales skills up a level. When you've asked your questions effectively, it will be time to implement the next step in the process.

Step 3. Listen constructively. Remember, one of the primary reasons you ask questions is to stimulate the customer to share information with you. If you're not good at accepting and processing that information, you've wasted the effort that you have expended to get that far. You need to be a good listener.

In many ways, it's more important to listen well than it is to speak well. Remember that you are a consultant. Your value to the customer begins with finding out what your customer wants or needs. You cannot discover that information if you don't listen to what your customer says. When your customer speaks, you'd better learn to listen well.

I intentionally use the words *listen constructively.* When you hear the word *construction,* you think of building or assembling something. That's what I mean to imply. It's your job to listen for things to build a relationship on and to build a sale on.

One of the best listening techniques involves programming your mind with some questions beforehand. This is a technique borrowed from speed-reading. A speed-reader first looks through a book's table of contents and then mentally asks questions about the contents. For example, looking through a book on sales techniques and finding a chapter titled "The Art of Asking Questions," you might ask yourself, "What good is asking questions?" or "What applications do questions have in sales?" or "How can I use questions?" With those questions loaded into your subconscious mind, as you skim through the words your mind seeks out the answers to those questions on a level beneath the conscious.

This technique can work for you. Prior to the sales call, load into your mind the questions you'd like to have answered; then, as you listen to the customer's responses, your mind will search for the answers to those questions.

Decide what kinds of things you're hoping to hear. Rehearse them in your mind and create a list. For example, before you enter into the interaction you might say to yourself, "I want to discover some things Lee does that I can connect with—things we have in common. I want to find out what the company's position is on this new technology, and whether there is anything I can do to influence the proposal I made last month that doesn't seem to be getting anywhere."

Now translate each of those objectives into a question. Your list might look like this:

"What do I have in common with Lee?"

"What is the company's position on the new technology?"

"What is their position on my last proposal?

"What would they like to see me change in my proposal in order for me to get the business?"

At this point you've loaded into your mind the questions you can use to construct a more solid relationship and to build a sale. You're prepared to listen constructively.

Listen for more than just words. Listen to the subjects your customer chooses to bring up. The things people choose to talk about are the things that are the most important to them.

Listen to what is *not* being said. Sometimes people intentionally talk around a subject that is too emotionally charged for them. For example, a customer might not want to mention the problems she's having with her current supplier if that supplier was her choice. Admitting the problems would be admitting her mistake.

Finally, notice your prospect's body language. It can reveal a whole dimension of attitudes and feelings that you may not be able to understand any other way.

Seven Rules for Constructive Listening

1. **Don't do all the talking.** Too many salespeople talk themselves out of sales by talking too much. The material you use to create a sale is not *your* conversation, it's your customer's conversation. If you're talking, your customer is not. Use the 75–25 rule of thumb. In other words, in every sales interaction, your customer should talk 75 percent of the time and you should talk 25 percent of the time.

2. **Don't interrupt when others are talking.** First, it's rude. Second, it's unwise. If you interrupt your customers before they're finished, you may never find out the things that they were in the process of telling you. You'll cut yourself off from valuable information.

3. **Don't start to argue or take exception before the person has finished.** Following this can be incredibly hard at times, but it's really a variation of the previous rule. It doesn't serve you well to interrupt your customers. It's always better to let them finish.

4. **Don't digress with a personal story all the time.** There are times to tell a personal story. It's a good way to connect with your customer, particularly early in a relationship. But it can get tedious if you do it all the time, and you can waste time and divert the conversation if you do it too often.

5. **Don't finish sentences for people.** It's rude and it causes frustration on the part of your customer.

6. **Don't wait impatiently for someone to finish so you can interject.** Generally, the person speaking will notice your impatience. That can be disconcerting to your customer. If you're fidgeting impatiently while you wait, both you and your customer know that you're not listening—you're thinking about what you want to say in response. You can't listen constructively while you're thinking about your comeback.

7. **Don't work too hard at maintaining eye contact.** You'll make people uncomfortable if you use unrelenting eye contact. You need to look away regularly to relieve the tension.

Step 4. Respond positively. You're not finished when you listen constructively. To be good at asking questions, you need to respond positively to every answer you receive. Don't ask the next question until you have responded to your customer's answer to the previous question.

Your ability to maintain an atmosphere that encourages your customer to answer additional questions rests in large measure on your skill in responding positively. You know that getting your customer to continue to answer questions is an absolute necessity if you are to successfully construct a sale.

When you respond to your customer, you send some verbal or nonverbal signal that you are listening and accepting what the customer has said. You don't necessarily have to agree with it, but you must let your customer know that his or her comments have registered with you.

Respond to everything. Every time your customer answers one of your questions, respond to that answer. Make sure that you respond to the answers positively. You can use body language like a nod of the head, or a facial expression such as a smile. The important thing is that your customer understands that you have heard and accepted what was said.

Paraphrasing what your customer says and feeding it back is a powerful response. Asking a thoughtful question about the answer is another. If nothing else, you can use verbal reinforcers like "Thanks," "Really," and "Oh" as a response, not as an interrogative.

After you've responded positively, you're back at the beginning of the cycle, ready to ask your next question. When you've asked the questions, gotten the information, and therefore gained a deeper and more useful knowledge of your customer, you've acquired the skills to become a master of the third hat, Effective Consultant.

Trying on the Third Hat

The third hat, Effective Consultant, focuses on principles and processes to help you gain a crucial understanding of the customer. The principles are:

1. *Your customers want to be understood.*
2. *Understanding your customer is like peeling an onion.*
3. *Generally, people will respond to you in the way you first behave toward them.*

The two key processes are:

• Preparing questions and
• Asking questions effectively.

When you master this set of competencies and apply them with discipline, your sales performance will take a quantum leap forward. Understanding the customer in depth and detail is 75 percent of the sales process.

But where do you begin?

Start small, focusing on one type of customer. For example, you might be selling industrial supplies to production supervisors, maintenance supervisors, and, in smaller shops, business owners themselves. Focus on one of those customer types and work through the process of preparing questions.

This is an area where some group brainstorming would be helpful. Talk to your manager about doing this exercise with several of your colleagues. A group in a brainstorming situation almost always produces better results than individuals working alone.

However, if you can't arrange that, then proceed on your own. Develop that set of questions for one market segment or customer type, and begin to use them. Before every sales call, review the steps in the process of using questions effectively. Work at improving your ability to set a comfortable atmosphere, probe into the customer's SPOO and PIE, and listen constructively.

As you feel yourself gaining competence with that customer type, repeat the entire process with another customer type. Build on your success, one customer type at a time. Incorporate what you've learned about the customers and about yourself into your preparation for the next customer type. Eventually, you'll be thoroughly prepared and very competent as you use your mastery of the third hat, Effective Consultant, to understand your customers and distance yourself from the competition.

Wearing the Third Hat

Imagine that you have mastered this hat to the point that you're one of the best practitioners of the third hat around. What would that look like?

You'll be extremely confident in your sales calls, whether you're calling on someone new or an old customer. That's because you'll have the experience and knowledge of this essential sales competency.

You'll find that this competency closely intertwines with the second hat, Trusted Friend. As you grow in your mastery of one of these hats, you'll find your results improving with the other. That's because there is a direct relationship between a customer's trust in you and the willingness to unveil information to you. As you develop a relationship with a customer, that customer shares more information. As that customer shares more information, the relationship grows. The net result is that you deepen your relationships with your customers as you improve your knowledge of them, a win–win situation.

You'll discover added confidence in all sorts of interpersonal situations, not just sales interactions. You'll discover that the best approach is almost always to ask questions first. If your child has a problem, if you have a disagreement with a friend, if the boss has an issue to discuss with you—in almost any situation, you'll discover the power and confidence that come from asking questions first. As that habit becomes ingrained, you'll find yourself becoming more and more effective in almost every personal interaction.

Finally, you'll watch your sales results improve almost magically. Your customers will respect and trust you, your presentations and proposals will be more focused, and you'll achieve greater results in less time. But, of course you knew that would happen. That's why you chose to master the third hat, Effective Consultant.

APPLICATION: USING THE SIX HATS TO TURN CHALLENGES INTO OPPORTUNITIES

Challenge: One of the highest-potential accounts in my territory has a very close relationship with one of my competitors. They are polite to me, but I can't get anywhere.

Although there is nothing new about this situation, it's becoming increasingly common. Think back to Chapter 1. Remember our discussion of turbulent times? Recall one of the key themes: Turbulent times affect your customers.

As a result of the pressures of our transition to the Information Age, your customers have less time and more pressure than before. One natural and common reaction, from their perspective, is to do more and more business with fewer and fewer vendors, and to build closer and closer relationships with them. This reduces the time they spend with salespeople, reduces their paperwork and administrative problems, and allows them to enjoy the kind of close relationships that allow them to shift some of the details and decisions onto their vendors.

That's a great situation if you're one of their chosen vendors. If you're on the outside looking in, that's not good. If you're a new salesperson or are representing a new company, this can be the situation you face most frequently. Almost every account you visit has existing relationships with your competitors. You'd better figure out how to resolve this situation or you won't have much of a future in sales. If you are an established salesperson with existing relationships, you might find your position in an account supplanted by a competitor.

I've been in both of those situations. As a new salesperson for a company that was expanding into a new geographical area, I had almost no business, and my competitors were the vendors of choice of every one of my accounts. Later, when I was an established representative, my largest account announced one day that the company's vice president had signed a prime vendor agreement with my largest competitor, and all of my business was going to be phased out over the next ninety days.

The circumstances surrounding the situation are of little importance. The reality is that if you're in one of these situations, you have a major problem. Your high-potential customer is committed to your competitor to some degree, and you still must sell to that account. That's a growing Information Age challenge.

APPLYING THE SIX HATS

Let's start with what *not* to do. Don't emphasize your Skillful Influencer (fourth hat) skills to continuously press your product or service or offer on your customers. Don't beat them over the head with the superiority of your product or service or offer. The exception, of course, is if your offer is so clearly superior and so obviously more advantageous that someone would risk losing a job by not buying from you. If that's the case, then you're probably wise to really push your product or service or offer; but that is rarely the case. It is likely that the differences between your offer and those of your competitors are probably not as great as they once were. Remember, growing competition is a characteristic of the Information Age.

Unless you've got a clear, outstanding, job-threatening advantage, don't push your product. In the minds of your customers, the issue isn't the product. To them, the issue is the relationship. Your customer is sophisticated enough to know that there isn't much difference between your offering and your competitor's, nor between your service and your competitor's, nor between your prices and your competitor's.

What should you do?

Put on your first hat (Astute Planner) again. This time, focus on the information collecting aspect. Dig around the edges of your competitor's business, trying to locate some small or marginal items that you could sell that your competitor doesn't sell. Don't go head-to-head with your competitor's strengths; you'll never win. Instead, try to find opportunities that do not infringe on your competitor's business or interfere with his or her relationship with the customer. You'll need all the information collecting skills encompassed by the Astute Planner hat.

If you're unable to find products that don't interfere with your competitor's relationships, try to find individuals on the margins of the business. Perhaps there are unaddressed departments or areas of the business that have been neglected. Those are the areas to focus on. Remember, your primary strategy is to find small, unobtrusive areas to get your product line in without threatening the relationship your competitor has with the customer. If you can find a small place to put your product, you'll create a reason to be in touch with the customer and you'll have an opportunity to build relationships.

At that point, you can put on hats number two (Trusted Friend) and three (Effective Consultant). Use your exposure in the account as a reason to build relationships. As you do, position yourself to be the vendor of choice when and if the competitor stumbles in providing service.

Here's another strategy that may fit your account. Use your Trusted Friend hat to identify an individual within the account company who is disgruntled with the competition. There is bound to be somebody, one decision maker or influencer, who will be more comfortable with you than with your competitor, someone who meshes with you more than with the competition. Then use your Effective Consultant skills to identify that individual's SPOO and PIE, and work your product into the account on an individual basis.

One last thought: Sometimes the best thing you can do is maintain a relationship, however superficial, with the key decision makers, and be patient. I recall being very frustrated with the situation at one of my key accounts when my competitor was firmly entrenched. As I was venting my frustration to my manager, he advised me to be patient, saying that the only thing I could count on was that things would change. My job was to maintain a relationship with the customer until something changed. At that point, I'd be positioned to take advantage of the change.

He was right. A year or so later, my competitor changed salespeople and the customer didn't like the new salesperson. The company made some service mistakes, and I had my opportunity. Within a short time, I became the primary vendor.

This is one of the most difficult Information Age selling situations. To be successful, you'll need to skillfully apply a number of hats, and hope that your competitor never reads this book!

THE FOURTH HAT:
SKILLFUL INFLUENCER

Welcome to the fourth hat, Skillful Influencer. I realize that some of you, looking at the word *influencer,* may have previously thought that this term describes what sales is all about. By now, however, you know that's not the case in the Information Age. Influencing your customer is just one of the six hats, not the whole of the job.

That's not to say that the skills and competencies encompassed by this hat are unimportant. They are incredibly important. After all, the final measurement of your success is money changing hands, and a major part of bringing that exchange about has to do with your skill at influencing people to do business with you. If your customers aren't saying "yes" to you in a regular fashion, you're going to be without a job soon. So you need to gain the skills and competencies required to influence people to give you money for what you offer.

In one sense, part of the contribution is made by several of the other hats. The second hat, Trusted Friend, and the third hat, Effective Consultant, both speak directly to your need to influence your customers. Having a positive influence is much easier and more effectively achieved when you engage both of those hats. They set the stage and precondition the customer to be receptive to what you're saying. Think of them as necessary but indirect.

When you put on the fourth hat, however, you're focusing specifically on your *direct* activity in moving your customer to take action on your behalf.

Selling is like basketball. At some point, you must put the ball in the basket. But you can't do that without developing the skills of dribbling, rebounding, and passing. Those skills are necessary but not sufficient. They get you to the point where you have an opportunity to put the ball in the basket. Presenting and closing, the skills we discuss in this chapter, are the equivalent of putting the ball in the basket.

That brings us to the first principle:

⚓ Deciding to buy is a process, consisting of a series of small decisions.

When your customers decide to give you money for what you're offering, that decision doesn't exist in a vacuum. The decision is only the latest in a string of decisions that your customer made along the way.

Let's illustrate with a simple selling situation. Suppose you're selling an expensive product to homeowners—water conditioners. Your company advertises in the phone books, occasionally on TV, and regularly in the newspapers. As a result, you are supplied with a good quantity of leads. When you attempt to sell a water conditioner, it is usually a one-call sales process, with the customers often deciding whether they are going to spend money with you while you are there with them. That's about as simple as a sales situation can be. Your own selling situation might be quite a bit more involved than that.

Now let's look at the process involved, from the customer's perspective, as the customer proceeds toward a decision to buy. For a change, we're not going to describe a process for you to follow, but rather one that customers generally follow.

Let's think in terms of the decisions a customer must make along the way. The first decision customers must make is whether or not to phone your company as a result of the advertisement. If they decide not to, you never hear of them. But some decide to call, and thus move one step forward in the process.

The next decision is one you probably haven't thought of. Customers need to decide whether or not to interact honestly with the person on the other end of the phone. Suppose you are in the office and you receive the call. In the first few moments of that call, the customer on the other end of the phone is making a subconscious decision as to how candid to be with you. You know that, because you've been in the same position when you've been the buyer. If the person on the other end of the phone is curt, abrasive, a know-it-all, or unconcerned about you, chances are you won't spend a lot of time describing your situation and asking questions. You'll brush the person off as best you can, and move on to someone else. So it is with your customers. In this situation, as in yours, they must make a decision to interact honestly with you before the sales process can go forward. That's the second decision in this simple sales process. Figure 9-1 illustrates the first two decisions.

FIGURE 9-1

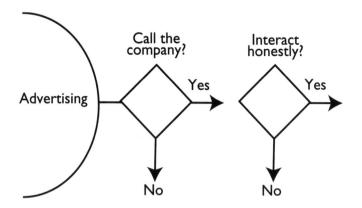

Customer Decisions in a Simplified Sales Process

Once a customer has decided to interact honestly with you, you're probably going to ask for an appointment. The third decision is whether to give you an appointment. Our diagram now looks like Figure 9-2.

FIGURE 9-2

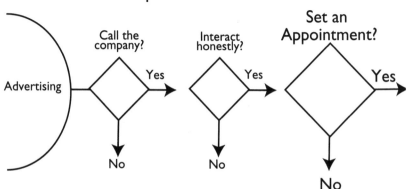

Customer Decisions in a Simplified Sales Process

What's the next decision? It's not whether to buy; you're getting too far ahead of things. The next decision customers make is whether or not to keep the appointment they made with you. I'm sure you've had lots of appointments that were broken by one side or the other. It's probably a weekly if not daily occurrence for some salespeople. If the customers don't keep the appointment, your time is wasted and your job complicated. Before you can influence them to spend money with you, you must influence them to keep the appointment. Now our diagram looks like Figure 9-3.

FIGURE 9-3

Customer Decisions in a
Simplified Sales Process

Let's suppose the customers have kept the appointment and you're entering their home. Both husband and wife are there to talk with you. Their next decision is similar to the one they made in the first few moments of the phone call: They need to decide whether to interact honestly and thoroughly with you. If they don't trust you or don't like you, or something about you makes them uncomfortable or suspicious, they won't want to deal with you.

In our home remodeling project, my wife and I had two electricians come to the house to estimate a significant piece of electrical work. The first was a very personable young man, the owner of a small electrical contracting business who came in the early evening, at the end of his workday. He was pleasant and knowledgeable, and even offered some ideas on how to do the job less expensively. He took the time to ask some good questions and got to know our requirements. He said he'd fax me a written estimate the next day, and he did so.

The next day, the second electrician called thirty-five minutes after he was supposed to arrive, saying he was delayed and would be late. He never apologized for being late. When he appeared, he had a bit of a sour attitude about him, and never smiled the whole time he was there. As I showed him the project, he made comments about how difficult it would be. Halfway through the conversation, I decided not to spend any more time with him. I never mentioned the complete list of items I wanted done, because I had already decided not to do business with him.

In the first few moments of his time with me, I made the decision not to interact honestly and thoroughly with him.

That's how your customers operate. Without a positive decision at this point, you'll never have an opportunity to get to the final decision. Our illustration now looks like Figure 9-4.

FIGURE 9-4

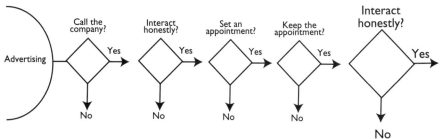

Customer Decisions in a
Simplified Sales Process

Finally, if you've successfully influenced your customers to make positive decisions along the way, you'll have the opportunity to present them with the final decision: whether to say yes or no to your offer (Figure 9-5).

This example describes a very simple selling situation. Yet even in this one-call closing situation, we've identified six specific decisions that customers must make in order for you to walk away with an order. Imagine how complex the process can be to purchase something like a new telephone system that affects almost every employee of the company, or a major piece of capital equipment that the production line revolves around.

FIGURE 9-5

Customer Decisions in a
Simplified Sales Process

Because the buying process is an involved series of small decisions, you must match that process with a process of your own.
Your job as a Skillfull Influencer is to facilitate the buying process
so that your customer finds it easy to say "yes" to you at each step
along the way. In order to do that, you need to master the fundamental process for influencing people to take action.

PROCESS: MANAGING AN
INTERACTIVE SALES DIALOGUE

The heart of the sales process is the conversation with your customers and prospects. It's that moment in time when you are face
to face with the customer that defines the uniqueness of your position and distinguishes you from all the others who work for your
company. If you're going to be a Skillful Influencer, you must master this process.

To begin, let's think about the most basic steps of the sales
process. We've looked at a simple sales process from the perspective of the buyer. Now let's look at a simple sales process from the
perspective of the seller—you. What you do when you speak with
your customers is this:

1. Make them comfortable with you.
2. Find out what they want.
3. Describe what you offer.
4. Show how what you have helps them get what they want.
5. Get their agreement to take the next step.

That simple five-step process is basic to every interaction you have with your customer. It's the heart of influencing. It can take months to complete in an intricate sales process, or it can be run through in two minutes over the phone. For example, in the initial phone call in our example, the decision is twofold: 1) whether to interact honestly and thoroughly with you, and 2) whether to make an appointment with you.

Your job is to facilitate those two decisions. So, you make the customers comfortable with you, which facilitates the first decision. Then you listen to their story, present the need for an appointment, and ask for the appointment. That facilitates the next decision. In this short two- to five-minute phone call, you've progressed through each of the five basic steps.

Let's think about a very complex, long-term sales process. Suppose you're selling production equipment with a price tag in the hundreds of thousands of dollars. Several of my clients are in this business. One of them, following my discussion of flowcharting sales processes, identified twenty-seven specific steps needed to go from the initial meeting to the final resolution of the sale. For the salesperson, each interaction with the customer provides an opportunity to progress through the five basic steps. My colleague's twenty-seven steps can be laid out in relation to the five steps, with each of the twenty-seven specific steps representing a small movement toward satisfying each of the five basic steps. For example, a salesperson might meet with the production supervisor to get that person's take on the intricacies of the equipment. Then the salesperson might meet with the current operators or supervisors to understand their perspectives. Next the salesperson might meet with the controller to understand the company's financing preferences and return on investment goals. Finally, the salesperson might meet with the purchasing agent handling the sale to gather that department's perspective. There are four specific meetings, four of the twenty-seven steps. Yet each one is a form of step two, "Find out what they want." In this case it could take weeks to complete that step.

This process is basic to every interaction you have with your customer. It's the heart of influencing. Let's examine the process and consider how to master it. When you master it, you'll be able to use it effectively, countless times throughout each day.

Several years ago, I would have described this process as *making a sales presentation*. But that term emphasizes one-way communication—you talking to the customer—and that's just not effective. Now I describe the process as *managing a sales interaction*. Here's why I've changed my terminology. *Managing* describes your major role. Your primary role is not as a presenter of information. Rather, your primary role is to manage the communication process between you and your customer. What happens between you and your customer is solely and entirely *your* responsibility. Just as managers are responsible for the processes in their departments, you are responsible for the communication process between you and your customer.

Interactive refers to the notion that the communication is two-way, not one-way. It consists of conversation between you and your customer. Without conversation from your customer, the sales process is not viable. Selling isn't telling. If anything, the more your customer talks and the less talking you do, the more effective the sales call will be.

Sales refers to the fact that the communication is moving toward an agreement between the two of you. When you're passing the time of day with your spouse or engaging in light banter at a cocktail party, you're not engaged in a sales dialogue. The purpose of the communication is not to come to an agreement. My definition of sales is this: *influencing a customer to come to an agreement with you to purchase something you offer.* The agreement is the main thing. The conversation is a sales conversation because it focuses on coming to an agreement.

Finally, the process is a *dialogue*. That means it's an honest exchange of feelings, facts, values, and perceptions. The depth and quality of that interaction and communication are the distinguishing standards.

Now that you understand the definition of the process, the question is, "How do you manage an interactive sales dialogue so that the chances of its success are enhanced?"

Let's start by comparing the process to a baseball game.

Figure 9-6 graphically describes the process. You know how baseball is played. If you're the batter, you start by taking your position in the on-deck circle. There you wait for your opportunity to go to bat. If you never get to the batter's box, you never have an opportunity to score.

If you're fortunate, you get to the batter's box. Now you have an opportunity to make a hit and score a run. If you're good and you make a hit, you run to first base. If you successfully negotiate first base, you then move to second base. From second you move to third. At this point, how many runs have you scored?

FIGURE 9-6

Process for Managing an Interactive Sales Dialogue

Obviously, none. Nothing counts until you make it to home. Now let's compare this process to our interactive sales dialogue. The steps in the baseball process correspond to the five basic steps of the sales process. In baseball, you first need to move from the on-deck circle to the batter's box. Study Figure 9-7.

In the sales process, you get to batting position when you put on your Trusted Friend hat and establish rapport with the customer, making the customer feel comfortable with you. Without doing that, you have very little opportunity to go further.

FIGURE 9-7

Process for Managing an
Interactive Sales Dialogue

3. Communicate the
features of your offering.

2. Understand
the customer.

4. Translate the
features into benefits
for the customer.

1. Help your customer
feel comfortable with you.

5. Acquire an
agreement for action.

Once you get to the batter's box, you next have to hit the ball and run to first base. First base in the sales process is understanding the customer's needs and interests. You'll use your third hat, Effective Consultant, to do that.

When you're playing baseball, you can't go to second base until you've made it to first safely. In sales, you can't talk about your product or service until you successfully understand your customer's needs. You accomplish this primarily by asking good questions and listening constructively.

Now you're ready to move to second base. You arrive at second base when you finally earn the opportunity to point out the features of your product or service. From that point you move quickly to third base, which requires you to translate those features into benefits.

Finally, to score a run, you have to safely negotiate home plate. In the sales process, that means that you successfully acquire an agreement from your customer for the next step, or the action that both of you will take as a result of your dialogue.

To a great degree, your success as a salesperson will be dependent on your ability to successfully manage interactive sales dialogues over and over again with your customers. Let's discuss each step of this process in detail.

Step 1: Get to the batter's box: Help your customer feel comfortable with you. Getting to the batter's box means that you have created a feeling of comfort and trust in the customer. That's a necessary prerequisite for going further. You don't get a chance even to take a swing unless you've done that.

The techniques we discussed in the chapters devoted to the second hat, Trusted Friend, come into play now. You employ those competencies in the early part of a sales dialogue to create comfort and interest. Reflecting your customer's style, showing interest, and connecting with your customer on a personal or business basis will be your primary strategies for helping the customer feel comfortable with you.

Step 2. First base: Understand your customer. Once you've achieved a comfort level, you can move on to the next step—getting to first base. In sales, that means understanding the customer. Put on hat number three, Effective Consultant, to achieve this.

This is the time to implement all the skills we discussed in Chapters 7 and 8. Use them effectively and you'll do a masterful job of getting to first base.

Step 3. Second base: Communicate the features of your offering. In baseball, once you've gotten to first base, your next goal is second base. In sales, once you've acquired an understand-

ing of your customer, it's time to present your product or service offering. We'll discuss this in detail shortly. In this analogy, presenting the features of your offering gets you successfully to second base.

Step 4. Third base: Translate features into benefits. From second base, third base is the goal. In sales, that means describing how your product or service offering will impact your customer. You now talk about the customer, not your offering. We'll discuss this in more detail shortly, also.

In the sales process, you successfully negotiate second and third base by mastering the competency of presenting.

Step 5. Home plate: Acquire an agreement for action. In baseball, nothing really matters until someone crosses home plate. Only then does the score change and all your effort count. In sales, nothing really matters until you get an agreement from the customer to take the next step. The next step could be anything from issuing a purchase order to agreeing to an appointment. The important thing is that your sales process is not successful until your customer agrees to some action.

Because we've already discussed the competencies involved in moving from the on-deck circle to the batter's box in previous chapters, let's focus now on presenting and closing, the two core competencies involved in mastering the Skillful Influencer hat. They are the skills you use to travel from first base to home plate. First we'll turn to presenting; then in Chapter 10 we'll discuss closing.

Presenting

⚓ *Presentations are always about two subjects: your offering and your customer.*

One of the most common mistakes salespeople make is this focusing the presentation exclusively on their offerings, forgetting to talk about the customer. It's a common mistake of both the greenest rookie and the most experienced professional. Product-focused selling is a vestige of days gone by.

Remember my experience in my first sales training session? Six weeks of memorizing a presentation, all about the features of the product I was selling. That was okay when times were slower, products and services were much more distinguishable from one another, and customers had more time. But it no longer works.

Today's Skillful Influencer must do the work for the customer, not only pointing out the features of the product or service but also translating those features into descriptions of how they will help the customer. Skillful presentations are, therefore, just as much about the person (that's the individual, department, or company to whom you're selling) as they are about your product or service.

To be effective, you need to sift through all the features of the product or service, select those that are most important, and relate them to the customer. Here's how you do that.

PROCESS: PRESENTING YOUR PRODUCT, SERVICE, OR OFFERING

Step 1. Describe your best understanding of the customer's objectives. Here's the best place to start a presentation, although very few salespeople ever do: Begin by restating what your customer wants to accomplish. After all, that is what your customer is interested in. It's the reason she's allowed you to be there, the reason he's invested time in you. Begin your presentation with a restatement of what your customer wants to achieve—the problems to be overcome or the objectives to be gained. I always prefer to present the customer with a written description of SPOO, but you might want to do this verbally.

After you have described the customer's SPOO and before you go any further, ask the customer whether you have accurately understood his or her position.

At this point the customer might say that yes, you have understood and accurately described the position. That's great. It means that you're beginning the presentation with a positive; the customer is saying yes to you. Also, you've already distanced yourself from your competitors because you're probably the only salesperson who cares enough to make sure you have accurately understood the customer. That will go a long way toward influencing your customer. The customer is impressed that you really do understand.

What if your customer says no, you haven't described the situation correctly?

It means one of two things. If you're completely off in your understanding of the customer, then you have no business describing your product or service or offer, because it was designed as a solution to your customer's SPOO. If your understanding of the customer is off, your solution will also be off. Stop, encourage your customer to more accurately describe the SPOO, and then make an appointment to come back later with a revised presentation.

It's more likely, however, that you won't have completely misunderstood the customer's SPOO; rather, you'll have missed the mark on one or two small issues. Allow your customer to correct you, thank him or her, and then restate your best understanding of the revised SPOO. If your customer now says Yes, then you've achieved the initial agreement and you can proceed with the presentation.

In either case, you eventually begin with a very positive step that differentiates you from the competition. With that accomplished, you can move into the discussion of what you have to offer as a means of helping your customer accomplish the SPOO.

Step 2. Identify the salient features of your product or service. Features are describable characteristics of your product, service, or offering. For example, if you're selling a mechanical pencil, you could talk about the size of the lead, the weight of the pencil, the color or shape, its material composition, where and how it was made, or its price. You could also talk about your company's inventory of the pencil, your history, how long you've been in the pencil selling business, or how many people have bought them from you. All these are features. Some are features of the product; others are features of your company, yourself, and your offering. All are part of the buying decision. Your customers don't just buy pencils. They buy them from an individual (you) and a company (your company). They buy them at a certain price with certain delivery arrangements and payment terms. All of these aspects are part of the buying decision and may be described to help the customer make a good decision.

When I'm teaching this module in a sales training session, I ask the participants to pick a product or service they sell and list ten features. When they're finished, I challenge them to double the number of features they've listed. When they're finished with that exercise, I often ask them to double again the number of features they've listed. It takes some creativity, but it can always be done. The point of the exercise is that you have far more things to talk about than you have time in which to do so. You can't possibly take the time to describe forty features of a product, of yourself, of your company, and of the offer, so you have to prioritize and only describe the features that are important to your customer.

How do you know which features they are? That's why you run to first base first. You've taken the time to understand your customers' SPOO and PIE, and now you can select the features that are most important to them.

Step 3. Communicate the features with detail and power.
Which of these two statements is more credible?

"It produces about a 50 percent return."

"It produces a 49.67 percent return."

If you're like most people, the second statement sounds more credible because of the detail. There is credibility and substance in accurate detail. Unfortunately, most salespeople are not detail-oriented. They've fallen into the habit of using general terms, and thereby forfeit much of the power of their presentations. I like to refer to statements like "... about 50 percent" as "salesperson's talk." Salesperson's talk is comprised of general, vague statements that are difficult to substantiate and are designed to be positive sounding.

Test yourself. If you were buying and were considering two proposals, which of these two statements would make you feel more comfortable and confident with the salesperson who makes the statement?

"It'll cost around $2,500.00."

"It'll cost $2, 511.27."

There is power in detail. Use it.

Adding detail is not the only way to add power to your presentation. Another way is to prepare third-party recommendations. They can be case studies, letters of recommendation, third-party studies, or lists of happy customers. These documents should be designed to support the credibility of what you're saying. Believe me, just because you say it doesn't mean that your customer believes it. If you can provide someone else to support your statement, you'll add power to your presentations.

Here's one other technique to add power to your presentations: Get your customer involved in the presentation as deeply and broadly as possible. If you're presenting a physical thing, for example, hand it to your customer to work the latches and flip the buttons. If you're presenting a service or a concept (like an insurance policy) have customers fill in the blanks for the calculations or add simple figures. The more your customers are involved, the more likely they are to believe what they've just encountered, and the more power you've built into the presentation.

Let's return to the example of the mechanical pencil. In order to add power to the presentation, you might want to hand your customer a pencil and say, "Here, take a look at it yourself." By doing so, you've involved your customer in the presentation and appealed to a source other than yourself to validate your statement. That source is your customer!

Step 4. Translate the features into specific benefits. When you translate a feature into a benefit, the subject of your sentence changes. When you're describing a feature, you talk about *it*. When you're describing a benefit, you talk about *your customer*. The subject of a feature sentence is the product or service. The subject of a benefit sentence is your customer.

Remember PIE: problems or objective, implications, and emotions. Your presentation should parallel those three levels. Features parallel problems or objectives, and benefits parallel implications and emotions. In other words, your benefits describe the positive effect your product will have on the implications and emotions the customer is concerned with.

Let's use the example of the mechanical pencil. You've described the extra long eraser contained inside the top of the pencil. That's the feature. It's a describable characteristic of the product. Then you translate that feature into a benefit that addresses one of your customer's implications. You say, "This means that you can erase a whole page of notes or a column of numbers without having to change erasers. You won't have to keep separate erasers on your desk, so you'll work more efficiently."

That's a benefit. It describes the implications for the customer. Note that the subject of the sentence is *you*. Here's a simple technique for translating features into benefits. Use the transitional phrase, "This means that you ...." Because it's a transition, your customer won't even notice the language; yet it helps you stick to the rule of changing the subject of the sentence.

Step 5. Render the benefits into descriptions of positive emotions. Remember PIE. You've addressed the problems and implications; now it's time to address the emotional level. Now you're going to render each of the benefits into descriptions of how that will make the customer feel. Going back to the mechanical pencil, you've just said, "This means that you can erase a whole page of notes or a column of numbers without having to change erasers. You won't have to keep separate erasers on your desk, so you'll work more efficiently." Now render that benefit into a description of a positive effect on your customer's emotions. Say something like this: "You won't be frustrated at having to search for extra erasers or aggravated at having to constantly switch from a pencil to an eraser."

And so you proceed through your selection of features, describing the feature, translating it into a benefit, and rendering the benefit into a description of a positive emotion.

You can use this inductive approach or flip-flop the sequence and use a deductive approach, reasoning from the end result or the emotion to the benefit, and from the benefit to the feature. Figure 9-8 illustrates the relationship between your earlier understanding of the customer's SPOO and PIE, and your presentation of your offering.

Presenting on the Next Level: Concepts and Philosophy

As your customers grow more and more weary of the pressures on them, they look for ways to reduce their stress and ease their time constraints. At some point, for some customers, the issue is no longer which product to buy. Rather, it's which company has the

FIGURE 9-8

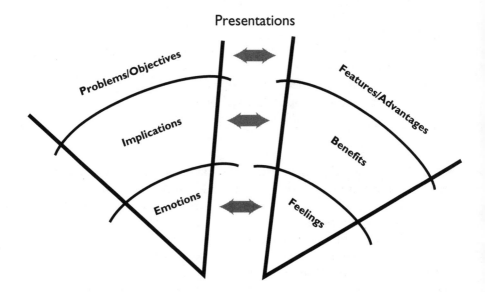

concept or philosophy that most compatibly matches theirs. That is a smart long-term strategy on their part.

A great example of this is our own experience with software. I'm sure you have a similar story. A number of years ago, back in the days of DOS, we had identified a need for a word processing program as well as a flexible database manager. Our search lead us to a great software package that was heavily promoted at the time. It was the highest-rated word processing program combined with the number-one-rated PC-based database program. We bought it, learned to use it, and standardized our office files on it.

It was a great product, perfect for our needs at the time. But we made a mistake by buying it. A few years later, we watched the growth of Windows-based applications. The company that sold our software eventually produced Windows versions of both programs, but it was clear they were losing interest in those products, deciding as a company to put their R& D money into other kinds of programs. We were stuck with an obsolete system.

We're smarter now. We've converted to a brand of software that we know is not the best on the market. However, we know the company is philosophically committed to continuously improving products for small businesses like mine. In the long term, we'll experience less hassle and lose less time because we bought from a company whose philosophy is compatible with who we are.

When you're presenting to your customers, don't think just about the product or service you offer. Think about the long-term benefit of positioning your company's philosophy in your customers' minds.

After you have completed your presentation, it is time to close the sale. That's what we'll discuss in Chapter 10.

10

SKILLFUL INFLUENCER: PART II

Let's momentarily review the baseball diamond—the basic influencing process. If you've progressed through the process to this point, you've helped your customer feel comfortable with you; that's getting to the batter's box. Then, through the skillful use of questions and constructive listening, you have understood the customer's SPOO and PIE. Congratulations. You skillfully achieved first base and distinguished yourself from your competition.

You made it around second and third bases by presenting your company, your company's philosophy, and your product and service. You carefully matched each salient feature to your customer's SPOO and PIE, translated them into benefits, and rendered them into descriptions of positive emotional impact. You've told and shown your customer why he or she should purchase your product.

You've reached third base. At this point, how many runs have you scored? Obviously, the answer is none. Nothing really counts until you have crossed home plate, and that means closing the sale.

Closing the Sale

When I ask salespeople to rate themselves on their competence at all the different parts of the sales process, they invariably rate themselves low at closing the sale. Unfortunately, salespeople who don't resolve the issues and get a decision from the customer waste time. There is no time to be wasted in the new environment. Being adept at closing the sale is an important key to productivity. Let's examine the issue of closing, beginning with the first principle:

⚓ *Closing is a process that always ends with your customer's agreement to take action.*

As you consider this principle, you'll realize that closing is not just asking for an order, although it certainly is that. In addition, it is a process you repeat at every stage of the sales process. In fact, almost every time you interact with a customer, you can close the interaction by asking for some agreement. Whenever your customer agrees to take some action, you have closed that step in the sales process.

Let's illustrate this principle with a typical real-life situation. Suppose you're talking on the phone to a prospect, who says, "Sounds interesting. Send me some literature." You say, "I'll put it in the mail today." Have you closed that step of the process?

The answer is no. You have agreed to take action—send some literature—but your prospect hasn't agreed to do anything. Remember, a close always ends with your customer agreeing to take some action.

Can you turn the same situation into a close? When your prospect says, "Sounds interesting. Send me some literature," you remark, "I'd be happy to. After you review it, will you discuss it with me over the phone, say next Friday?" If your customer says yes, you've closed. The customer has agreed to take some action.

Understanding this principle is crucial to closing the sale. Many of the offers and proposals on which you work are very involved, requiring a number of steps in the sales process. As you proceed through the sales process, you continually ask for some kind of action in order to keep the project moving forward. When it comes time for the final decision—the agreement to buy—that decision is often the natural, logical consequence of the decisions that led up to it.

Closing, then, is not an isolated event that only happens at the end of the sales process. It's a routine part of every sales call. That leads us to the second powerful principle of closing the sale:

⚓ *Every interaction can and should be closed.*

In other words, at the conclusion of *every* interaction with your customer, ask for agreement on the action he or she will take.

The sample telephone conversation is a good example of closing the interaction. Here's another common situation. Suppose you've discussed a product or proposal with your customer, who says, "It looks interesting, but we're not ready for that now." You might then say, "When do you think will be a good time?" Your customer responds, "Probably around June." You might typically say, "I'll make a note to discuss it with you then." At this point, you haven't closed the interaction, nor have you resolved the issue.

Let's take the conversation one step further. Suppose you now say, "At that point in time, will you spend half an hour with me to discuss it in detail?" You have now attempted to close the interaction by getting an agreement for action on the part of your customer. You've put the issue on the table and are attempting to resolve it.

Suppose your customer says, "No, probably not." You now have a decision to make. Should you probe the reasons why, or should you accept the decision? If you decide to accept the decision, the conversation has value to you in that you learned that this proposal isn't going to fly with this account. The early "no" is valuable to you. You won't waste months chasing something that isn't going to happen. That's the value in resolving the issue.

Suppose your prospect responds to your close by saying, "Yeah, I think it has enough merit to spend that time discussing it with you." You now have a commitment to spend some time with you, so you have moved the issue forward. You're one step closer to the ultimate sale.

Implement these two principles and you'll dramatically improve your productivity. Keep in mind that closing is an agreement for action on the part of your customer, and make it your goal to close every interaction.

THE CLOSING PROCESS

Closing is, at least on the surface, a simple two- or three-step process:

1. Ask for action.
2. Respond appropriately.
3. If necessary, ask again.

In order to take the mystery out of the process and make it more comfortable for everyone, we're going to diagram the process in more detail. Study Figure 10-1, which illustrates the dynamics of the closing process.

FIGURE 10-1

THE DYNAMICS OF THE CLOSING PROCESS

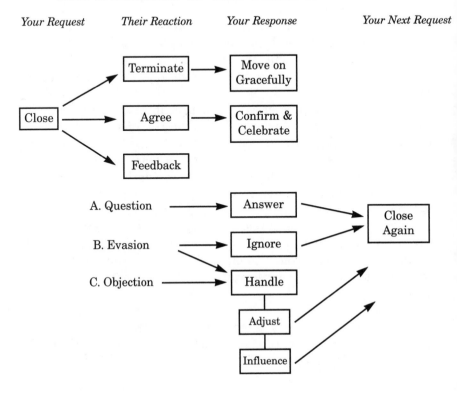

Your Request   *Their Reaction*   *Your Response*   *Your Next Request*

Step 1. Ask for action. The closing process begins when you ask your customer for some action. If you never put the issue on the table and ask for some action, you'll rarely close the sale. Certainly some customers will close the sale for you, and some sales will close in spite of you. But *you* won't close them unless you ask for action.

The closing process begins when you ask your customer to take action. When you make a request, your prospect reacts to your request. There are only a limited number of ways in which your customer can react. As Figure 10-1 shows, your customer can terminate, agree, or offer feedback. By definition, everything he or she says can be fit into one of those three categories. Let's look at each one.

The customer can terminate the conversation by telling you definitely, absolutely, without question, "No!" I call that the "terminal no" as opposed to a "tentative no."

It's very important for you to be able to distinguish a terminal no from a tentative no. A tentative no is when the customer says no, but really means something like "probably not" or "maybe."

I recall one of my most memorable illustrations of this principle. It was my first visit to an account that had been assigned to me. I was able to meet with the Materials Manager, a crusty older man who delighted in making salespeople squirm. I made my introductory pitch to him, and he responded with this comment: "Young man, we have too many vendors right now. We're trying to reduce the number of vendors we have. So we're not interested in dealing with someone new. Secondly, we don't know much about your company. But what we do know, we don't like. So I'd advise you not to waste your time here."

I interpreted that as a tentative no, not a terminal no. Several weeks later I went back to see him again. This time, I thought I'd play my strongest card by presenting a product that almost every hospital in the state bought from us—suction tubing. Suction tubing is a staple item in a hospital; it is used by every hospital in a number of different departments. At the time we had an arrangement with the premier manufacturer, guaranteeing us the best prices in the state. Almost every other hospital bought tubing from us. I was sure this customer had to buy my suction tubing deal.

After I presented the offer to him, he sighed and said, "We don't use any." I turned in my chair and looked into the hallway outside his office. There was a cart with some suction tubing hanging from it. Telling me they didn't use suction tubing was like saying they had no beds in their hospital. He was lying; I knew it and he knew it.

I chose to interpret that as a tentative no, not a terminal no. As luck would have it, several months later, I was able to find a buyer in the hospital with whom I could work. I discovered a tiny opening when one of their suppliers let them down, and I was given an opportunity to bring in a product. We did well with that line, and one thing led to another. Within three years, that account had grown so much that it became the hospital in which I had the greatest penetration of all my accounts.

All because I was able to distinguish between a tentative no and a terminal no.

Of course, there's always the possibility that your customer will agree to your request. Good for you. When your customer agrees to take some action, you've closed!

Enjoy it.

The most common response, however, is to offer some feedback. There are only three kinds of feedback. By definition, every possible word out of the customer's mouth will fit into one of these three categories: question, evasion, or objection.

You know what a question is. An evasion is when your prospect makes a comment that suggests unwillingness to commit to any position. The classic, "I want to think about it," is an example. An objection is a reason for not doing what you want your prospect to do. Once your prospect has reacted, it's time for you to respond to the reaction.

Step 2. Respond appropriately. Let's think about each of these possibilities. If the customer terminates, what is your most appropriate response? Move on gracefully. Don't get angry, and don't slam the door or call anyone names. You never know when that person will surface again at some other account. Move on gracefully, remembering the first law of sales: You don't sell them all.

If the customer agrees, confirm the agreement and then celebrate! Good for you; you got one. Enjoy the burst of pleasure that gives you. It's one of the reasons you're a salesperson. There is a certain satisfaction, a high that comes from getting agreement, especially on a big deal, that is a special fringe benefit of selling.

Let's look at feedback. If your customer asks you a question, what do you do? Answer the question. That's simple enough.

If she evades your question, you have two appropriate choices. The first is to ignore her evasive comment. That's right, ignore it. I remember hearing a sales trainer some years ago talk about ignoring a customer's first evasion. He said that the first time people offer an evasion, they are merely processing the issue in their minds and don't really mean what they say. So it's often best to ignore it and go on.

Suppose you ask the question, "Should we go ahead with this?" and your prospect says, "I'd like to think about it a little." Your response is, "Should we deliver it Monday, or is Tuesday better?" You've totally ignored the comment.

I have found this technique works once—for their first evasion. But don't do it more than once in an interaction.

The other choice is to handle your customer's objection.

HANDLING OBJECTIONS

Now you're dealing with an objection, a reason to say no. It should
come as no surprise to you that the best way to handle an objection
is with a process. Here it is.

Step 1. Empathize. Begin by empathizing with your customer.
That takes some of the tension out of the situation, defuses any
defensiveness on his part, and builds a positive atmosphere.
Empathizing requires you to do two things. First, make a statement indicating that you understand how the prospect thinks or
feels. Second, support that statement with some proof. Your proof
is the reason he should believe that you really do understand how
he thinks or feels.

Here's an example. Your prospect has said, "I want to think it
over." You respond by empathizing. You say, "I know how you feel."
(That's your empathizing statement.) "Many of my other customers
responded the same way when they were first presented with this
concept." (That's your proof.)

Step 2. Probe. Once you've empathized with your customer, then
ask questions. Usually when you're responding to an objection or
evasion, the issue is too general to deal with effectively. Often your
customer hasn't accurately articulated the thoughts in her own
mind. Your questions, therefore, should be of the type that require
your customer to think more specifically. You must take her answer
from the vague and general to the specific. You can't respond to a
vague comment, but you can respond to a specific one. The primary
tool for moving your prospect from general to specific thoughts is a
good question.

In our example, after you've empathized, you ask, "When you
say that you want to think about it, what specifically is it that you
need to consider more deeply?"

Note that the question asks the prospect to think more specifically—to move from the general to the particular.

Step 3. Verify. When he answers, you then rephrase the answer and feed it back to him, confirming that it really is the way he thinks or feels. In the example, he says, "Well, Pat, I'm not sure about the price. It's more than we had planned in the budget. I'm not sure we want to pay that much." That would be a great answer, because it reveals the specific issue that is bothering the prospect.

Your skillful empathizing and questioning have uncovered the real problem. Now, you simply rephrase it and ask him to confirm what you've said. Your response could go like this: "In other words, you're concerned about how you can pay for it when it's more than what you had budgeted. Is that right?" When your prospect confirms it, you have successfully probed and clarified the evasion or objection to the point that you've moved from the general to the specific. Now you can deal with it.

As long as the prospect maintains that he "just wants to think about it," there is little you can do to move the project forward. But now that you understand exactly what the issue is, you can respond to the objection.

Step 4. Respond. You've clarified your prospect's evasion or objection to the point that it's a specific, understandable issue. Now what?

You respond in one of two ways. The first option is to adjust your proposal or presentation to your improved understanding of your prospect's situation and perception. In other words, you change. If your prospect says, "It's two dollars too much," then you have the choice of saying, "For you, we'll drop the price by two dollars." You've changed your proposal to meet your revised understanding of your prospect.

The second option is to respond to the objection in such a way as to influence your prospect to change. That means that you must get her to think differently.

How you do this can vary tremendously by the type of objection your prospect has raised. An unlimited number of objections can be raised, and you can make an unlimited number of responses to them. Rather than attempt to identify a hundred different strategies, I'd prefer to show you a process you can use to create your own responses.

PROCESS FOR PREPARING TO HANDLE OBJECTIONS

The secret is to *prepare* for your most likely objections. Remember the principle behind the Astute Planner hat: **You'll always be more effective if you think about what you do before you do it.** That principle applies here, also. In order to prepare, use this process.

Step 1. Identify the most common objections you hear. For any product or service you offer, there are five or six most common objections you will hear. If you can anticipate what those objections will be, you'll complete step one of the process.

Step 2. Outline a response. Having identified each of the most common objections, think about the most effective way to respond when you do hear them.

Here's an example. Your prospect has said, after you have probed and clarified, "It costs too much." As you think about responding to this objection, you decide that the first thing you're going to do is empathize once again.

You put a number one on your outline and write in "Empathize." Then you decide you need to find out how much is too much. So you pencil in a number two and write, "Ask how much is too much."

Next, you decide to restate the benefits of your proposal to the customer. You write the number three and write, "Restate the benefits." Then you decide to translate the "too much" amount into the least way of expressing it. In other words, if it's $500 too much for a yearlong time period, then it's really only about $1.35 a day too much. So item number four becomes, "Translate into lowest expression."

Next, compare the benefits to that low expression. Write down next to number five, "Compare benefits to lowest expression."

Finally, you decide to close again; that goes on the last line of our outline.

What you have now is an outline of the steps you want to follow when you hear this objection. But you're not finished yet.

Step 3. Acquire your ammunition. Gather the ammunition you'll need to support your position. Ammunition is anything you can use to support your statements. For example, do you have any third-party studies that confirm the benefits you've described, or any testimonials or articles from trade journals? That's all ammunition. Gather that kind of documentation and have it in your briefcase, ready to use when you meet your prospect's objections.

That brings us to the last column in Figure 10-1, and the last step of our larger closing process.

BACK TO THE CLOSING PROCESS

Step 3. Close again. "Close again" means that, after you have responded to your customer's statement, you once again make a request for your customer's action. That starts the whole process all over again.

Team Decisions

How do you close the sale when the decision is made by a team or committee, and you can't be there when they make the decision?

This situation is growing more and more common as the trend toward Total Quality Management programs spreads and teams do more of the decision making that was previously the job of individuals. In this situation, I'm going to assume that you've done a thorough job of selling. In other words, you have reached all the available team members, talked with them individually, understood their SPOO and PIE, and made a coherent, powerful presentation of your best solution to their problems and objectives. If you haven't done that, then you need to go back and do it first, before you attempt to bring the issue to closure.

Let's assume that you have finished selling, and the team is going to make a decision. What do you do? Here's the most effective approach. Find the team member you think is most strongly in favor of your solution, and ask him or her to advocate it to the team. Your request for action is not, "Will you buy this?" Rather, the issue you put before that team member is, "Will you recommend this?"

If you can get one strong team member on your side and willing to argue for you, your chances of closing that sale will be dramatically enhanced.

Alternate Next Steps

Much of the literature about closing works on the assumption that the person to whom you're speaking is the decision maker and has the authority to make the decision while you're present. However, this situation is growing increasingly less frequent. Many organizations are adopting policies and procedures that require multiple sign-offs on a decision or team approaches. It's inappropriate for you to ask for the order when your prospect does not have the appropriate authority.

In this situation, it's important that you develop alternate next steps. While you might want the purchase order, your buyer might not be able to give it to you for reasons that are totally beyond your ability to influence. Your best strategy is to back off and ask for something that isn't quite as difficult. I call that "preparing an alternate next step."

Here's an example. I once had a CPA firm as a client. The firm wanted to acquire additional customers for its computerized bookkeeping service. We developed a sales and marketing system that put them in front of a number of qualified prospects. At the first sales call, they asked the prospect to sign up for their bookkeeping service.

Think back to the discussion of risk and relationship in Chapter 5. Giving someone your bookkeeping business is a high-risk decision. Few prospects were ready to do that on the strength of just one sales call. When it became apparent that someone was not going to say yes to the major proposal, the salespeople were prepared with a fallback position. The fallback position was to ask the prospect for a set of financial statements so that the CPA firm could prepare a sample of what the computerized report would look like, using the prospect company's own figures. This alternate next step kept the proposal alive and moving forward while at the same time recognizing that some people were legitimately not ready to say yes to the big deal.

One of the best ways to prepare for closing is to think through each of your closing situations and prepare one or two alternate next steps that allow your prospect or customer to say yes to you and keep the project moving forward.

Master these processes and you'll gain the magic of the fourth hat: Skillful Influencer.

Trying on the Fourth Hat

The task of acquiring the magic of the fourth hat may seem overwhelming. After all, there were four powerful principles:

1. *Deciding to buy is a process, consisting of a series of small decisions.*
2. *Presentations are always about two subjects: your offering and your customer.*
3. *Closing is a process that always ends with your customer's agreement to take action.*
4. *Every interaction can and should be closed.*

These are some of the most powerful and useful principles for the Six-Hat Salesperson, addressing the very heart of the salesperson's job. In addition, this hat contains some of the most frequently used and most intricate processes. They were:

- The "managing an interactive sales dialogue" process
- The presentation process
- The closing process
- The handling objections process
- Preparing to handle objections process

It's no wonder you may be feeling a bit overwhelmed. As always, however, you can make the magic of the fourth hat yours by taking one small step at a time, and by building on your successes.

Where do you start? At the end, with closing. Learn two all-purpose closing questions.

"Where do we go from here?"

"What's the next step?"

Then use one of those closes at the end of every interaction with a customer: a phone call, an information collecting call, a service call—it doesn't matter. Discipline yourself to form the habit of asking for an agreement for action at the end of every conversation.

You'll be amazed at what this little change will do for you. You'll find yourself pushing projects forward that would otherwise have been stalled. You'll also find yourself resolving issues and moving on when before those issues would have been left simmering on the back burner for months. Later, as you gain confidence in that simple closing technique, you can build on your success and develop more sophisticated closes.

As soon as you achieve some comfort with the closing questions, focus on your presentations. Take some time to think about a presentation that you're scheduled to make. Rearrange it so that it fits the presentation process described earlier. Then practice it a time or two so that you're comfortable with it, and try it out.

A group approach to this issue may be of more benefit to you. Suggest a group brainstorming session to your manager. If you can arrange that, great. If not, push forward on your own.

As you become comfortable with the format for one product, spend that same amount of preparation time on all of your other products and services, moving from those most commonly presented first to those least commonly presented last. Eventually you'll find that the presentation process has become second nature to you.

At that point, you'll be well on your way to mastering the fourth hat: Skillful Influencer.

Wearing the Fourth Hat

What happens when you've mastered this hat's principles, processes, and tools so that they are habits, and you don't need to think about them anymore?

Your sales dollars per opportunity identified will dramatically improve. You'll be known throughout your company as the salesperson who wrings more dollars out of an account than anyone else. It's easy to understand why that will be true.

You'll be more effective in every contact you have with your customers, turning almost every conversation into a step in a constantly moving, positive process. As a result of your penchant for moving projects forward, your customers will come to respect and rely on you more, because they will know that things seems to get done when you're involved.

You will have practiced and used the presentation process so often that you won't have to think about it anymore; it'll be routine. Every now and then, you'll take the time to analyze your presentation for a new product, program, or service to make sure that you're continuing to adhere to the process and not getting sloppy. Every time your company develops a new product or service to sell, you'll organize the presentation in terms of the baseball diamond analogy, and practice making a presentation.

For every new offering, you'll also spend a couple of hours working through the process for preparing to handle objections. That work will pay dividends to you in multiples. In fact, you'll be closing at a far better rate than anyone else.

The confidence that brings you will spill over into every aspect of your job, all because you've truly become a master of the fourth hat: Skillful Influencer.

Application: Using the Six Hats to Turn Challenges into Opportunities

Challenge: My customers are confused because they have more choices than ever before. It's difficult to get them to make decisions.

Reflect for a moment on Chapter 1, where we discussed turbulent times. It's easy to see why this is a commonly occurring phenomenon of the Information Age. In the same way that the white water in a river is the most superficial indication of the rocks that lie beneath the surface, the confusion your customers feel is the symptom of some of the trends that lie beneath the surface of the global economy.

As more and more information becomes available, our customers become overwhelmed and confused by it. Technology creates new options, and new competitors spring up, vying for their business. Should they search the Internet for your product or service, respond to the people who are sending them catalogs in the mail, try that new competitor who is calling on them all the time, or stick to their old standby? No wonder they are confused.

Complexity and change are also on the increase on the insides of their businesses. It often seems that their own needs and applications are moving targets. They might need a new piece of equipment to assist in the production of a product today, but what if that product changes tomorrow? Can you blame them for hesitating to make a decision?

As always, your customers' confusion and uncertainty provide both an obstacle and an opportunity for you. It's an obstacle because it causes them to be uncertain and hesitant to make decisions. It's an opportunity because they are just as uncertain and confused about your competitor's offer as they are about yours. If you can figure out how to help them make those decisions, you'll gain a significant competitive edge.

APPLYING THE SIX HATS

You can use two hats to handle this challenge effectively—the second hat, Trusted Friend, and the third hat, Effective Consultant.

Let me illustrate from my own experience as a buyer. In my business, we have a continuous need for graphic design services as well as for audio and video production services. I regularly revise our promotional materials to meet the requirements of a constantly changing market. What looks good and is right today can be hopelessly obsolete in just a few weeks or months. At any point in time, I'm very hesitant to say yes to a new brochure or graphic design. It could be obsolete momentarily.

I've solved this headache by developing a relationship with a graphic designer who is responsive to all our changes and sensitive to our time needs. If we do want to change a design or a brochure three weeks after we last changed it, we can count on the relationship with the designer to easily facilitate those changes. The relationship is more important than any one particular design.

We could probably entertain a dozen proposals from a dozen different designers for each project. Certainly the chances are slim that our regular designer will have the outstanding design for each of the projects. The odds would be eleven to one against him.

But that's not the point. The relationship, the ability to change and be sensitive to our needs and keep us up to date on the latest techniques and methods, is far more important than any one design. Over a period of time, we're far better off building a working relationship with a competent person we can trust than we are taking any other course. As a seller, when you find a customer hesitant to make a decision, it may very well be because you're focusing on the product or service you're offering, and your customers are concerned about the likelihood of an ongoing relationship.

In the area of audio and video production, we have a need to regularly create multimedia training products. Sometimes they are video projects, sometimes audio, and sometimes combination projects. Sometimes they are done for our own product catalog, and sometimes they are produced under contract for a specific client.

Again, we could put each of these projects out for proposals. Our city is full of audio and video producers. We could probably get a dozen people to develop proposals for us. The likelihood of our regular suppliers always having the outstanding proposal is small. But, again, the ongoing relationship is more important than the individual proposal.

From our perspective as buyers, life is easier if we can work with a competent person we trust. While we understand that every project may not be absolutely the most creative and outstanding, we also understand that the body of work produced will certainly match anyone's standards. More important than any one project is the ability to easily communicate with and trust people who will be responsive to our needs and capable of changing to meet them.

My motivations and concerns as a buyer are similar to your customers'. As we are swept along by the turbulent tides of the Information Age, it's more and more important to find anchors that we can rely on. In a buyer–seller context, relationships can be those anchors.

The moral of the story? Take seriously the principles and processes encompassed by the second hat, Trusted Friend, and build solid relationships with your key customers. Help them to see you and your company as "competent people they can trust." If the relationship is intact, the decision to buy becomes easy. Remember our discussion of risk and relationship? The deeper the relationship you have with your customer, the less is the perceived risk in the mind of the customer. Build solid relationships, and your customers will make decisions more quickly.

At the same time you are building relationships, work at offering value to your customers by implementing the third hat, Effective Consultant. Pay particular attention to knowing your customers by peeling the onion. The deeper your understanding of your customers' situations, their SPOO and PIE, the more likely it is that you'll present them with proposals that will be easy for them to accept. When decisions are difficult for your customers, it is often because there is some unknown variable. If you do the best job of understanding your customers' SPOO and PIE, and the best job of presenting solutions to your customers, your proposals will make it easier for them to make decisions. You will have addressed all your customers' concerns thoroughly.

The issue isn't what you do, it's how well you do it. Distinguish yourself from your competition by being better than anyone else at implementing the competencies of the Six-Hat Salesperson, and you'll find your customers making decisions easily and quickly.

THE FIFTH HAT: ADEPT HUMAN RESOURCES MANAGER

The position of human resources manager came into prominence in the decades of the 1980s and 1990s as companies began to understand that one of their greatest assets was the group of human beings who worked for them—their employees. That realization coincided with the spread of the human potential movement, which proclaimed belief in the untapped, limitless potential of human beings. Hundreds of books and articles were and continue to be written to urge the readers to greater heights of achievement. Motivational speakers now crisscross the globe, urging their audiences to tap into their potential to achieve success.

It's not difficult to see how these two trends intersect. If human beings have the huge, untapped potential for success and achievement the motivators claim, then the wise company will develop a climate where the unleashing of that potential can take place. It's to the company's benefit. A human resources director is often the executive in charge of maximizing the company's human resources.

"So," you're thinking, "what does this have to do with sales or with me?"

If you're a human being, you have a vast reservoir of untapped potential.

If you can learn how to unleash more of that potential, your career will soar. Who is in charge of managing you in such a way as to unleash your potential? You've got it! You are!

Welcome to the fifth hat, Adept Human Resources Manager. The human resources you manage is *you*. When you put on this hat, you work with principles and processes that unleash your potential, so you're working at continuously increasing levels of effectiveness.

It took me about six months in my first full-time professional selling position to realize that much of my challenge as a salesperson resided inside my head, not out in the external world. Like the average outside salesperson, I spent only about one-third of my workweek actually face-to-face with customers. That's probably true of you, too. With whom do you spend the rest of your time? More than anyone else, with yourself. That means that if you are going to be successful in the Information Age, you must learn to get along with yourself. You must learn how to unleash your potential, maximize your human assets, and eliminate the obstacles that hinder your performance.

You must learn to unleash your potential, overcome adversity, deal with procrastination, and handle rejection and depression. Failing to do so will have a serious negative impact on your performance. It doesn't matter how smoothly you interact with your customers if you can't manage yourself.

To become a master of this hat, you'll need to master positive, proactive principles that help you reach your potential and overcome the negative hindrances that drag down your performance. Here's the first principle:

⚓ *You are always more effective when you set goals.*

One of the most effective strategies for getting the most out of yourself is to develop the habit of regularly setting powerful, motivating goals. Goals compel you to work with discipline and focus rather than going about your job mindlessly and routinely.

This doesn't mean that you can't do your job without goals. You can, and many salespeople do. But the discipline of goal setting forces you to think about what you do before you do it. It moves you out of the realm of being reactive, doing what other people want you to do, toward being proactive, doing what you want to do.

Goals provide focus and direction to your activities, and supply the motivation to push yourself beyond your comfort level. For example, if you're producing at a rate that provides you with a comfortable living, you may be content with your situation. Because you're content, you probably aren't going to grow and change; there is no reason to do so. However, if you commit to a goal of "increasing my business and therefore my income by 20 percent," then you've got to stretch yourself out of your current patterns of behavior to reach that goal. The goal is the device that prompts you to stretch yourself and to focus your efforts.

Goal setting is the beginning point in taking control of your job (and, in the same way, in taking control of your life). It is possible to go about your job in a purely reactive way. You can visit all your customers on a route-type basis, taking care of their problems and responding to their issues. Your day will be determined not so much by what you want to accomplish as by the problems and demands of your customers.

Look at Figure 11-1. It depicts a spectrum that describes the styles of doing your job.

FIGURE 11-1

At the far left end of the spectrum is the purely reactive style. The person who is purely reactive starts the day with no plan other than to see that day's customers in reply to that day's inquiries. He has no sales goals, seeking only to respond to what his customers ask for. He mindlessly goes through his days, weeks, months, and years responding only to other people's requests.

On the far right is the salesperson who is so proactive that she refuses to return phone calls if they aren't on the agenda.

While straying too close to either end of the spectrum can be a problem, it's been my experience that most salespeople tend to cluster toward the reactive end of the spectrum. As a result, they are not nearly as effective as they could be.

If you look at the spectrum, it's obvious that the fundamental difference between the salespeople on the left and those on the right is the presence or absence of goals. You can't be proactive and work your agenda unless you have an agenda. An agenda is a plan to achieve some end, and that end is a goal. An agenda begins with a powerful set of goals. The first step, then, in moving from reactive to proactive is to create a set of goals.

If you want to become an effective human resources manager, wringing the most out of yourself, a powerful set of motivating goals is the starting point.

Goal setting is much more than just an occasional exercise. Rather, it's a disciplined way of thinking about your job and your life that takes you from being reactive to becoming proactive. Think of it as a mind-set, not as a task. You'll need to build it into your life on a regular basis. Every year or so, review and refine your long-term (lifetime) goals and create a set of annual goals. Every few months, review your short-term goals. Regularly create monthly, weekly, and daily goals.

Regardless of what level you're working on, the process is always the same. Here are the steps you need to master to become an effective goal setter:

THE GOAL SETTING PROCESS

Step 1. Select an area on which to concentrate. The area can range from the very deep and foundational to the very specific and superficial. For example, you might want to focus on your spiritual growth. That's a deep and foundational area. Or you might want to focus on something much more specific, like the state of repair of your home. Regardless, you must begin by selecting an area of your life or your job on which to focus.

Step 2. Select the time period. Lifetime goals give purpose and definition to your life. Long-term goals span eight to twelve years in time. Mid-term goals address the time period from one to eight years in the future. Short-term goals can be for any period from a week to a year.

Let's say that you want to work on annual goals for the financial aspect of your life. You've identified the area (financial) and the time period (annual). You're now ready for the next step.

Step 3. Brainstorm (daydream) to create a list. Now you're going to create a long list of possibilities. You do this by looking at both the "gain" and the "pain" in the area you've selected. "Gain"

means focusing on the positive things that you'd like to have; "pain" means focusing on the negative things that you would like to be rid of.

To focus on the "gain," daydream about what you'd like to achieve with respect to that part of your life. Kick back, relax, and begin to list on a piece of paper all the things you'd like to accomplish in the area you're working on. Ask yourself these three questions:

- What would I like to be?
- What would I like to do?
- What would I like to have?

Create a list of your dreams. Don't edit or judge what you've written; rather, just make a long list of your dreams. No one else can do this for you because no one knows your situation and your aspirations better than you do.

Suppose you write these things down:

"Make a lot more money."

"Buy a new car."

"Put aside $2,000 in a retirement account."

"Save some money for the children's education."

You've created a list of possible annual goals for the financial aspect of your life.

Now look at the "pain" side of the issue. What problems do you have that you'd like to solve? Make a list. Then select from that list one or two items to start with. Let's say, for example, that your list contains two sales problems that you want to solve: "Stop wasting time," and "Stop losing potential new accounts to competitors."

Let's turn these problems into goals or objectives. It's easy. Just rewrite each problem as an objective, beginning with the word "to." "Stop wasting time" becomes "To stop wasting my time," and "Stop losing potential new accounts to competitors" becomes "To stop losing potential new accounts to competitors."

Now let's work with these statements in one more way. Let's turn the negative statement into a positive statement. Instead of saying "I want to stop wasting time," say, "I want to make better use of my time." Instead of saying, "I want to stop losing potential new accounts to competitors" say, "I want to gain new accounts."

It's amazing what this little change in language can do for you. Human nature is such that our minds are much more excited and active about pursuing a potential gain than about eliminating a problem. Rewriting your statement into a positive objective channels and unleashes your mental powers. Now you're ready for the next step.

Step 4. Prioritize. If you've done a good job daydreaming, you probably have a long list of things you'd like to accomplish. Unfortunately, you can't do everything. You just don't have enough time and energy to do everything you'd like to do. You must prioritize and select the things that are most important to you.

There's no formula for this other than to think carefully about each of your daydreams, compare them to your current situation, and select those that you feel are the most important to you. Remember to apply a dose of realism to this process. If you want to make $75,000 next year, for example, but you're currently in an $18,000 customer service position, that goal may not be very realistic.

Let's say you decide that your two most important goals for the year are to make a lot more money and to save some money for your children's education.

Step 5. Specify. This step requires you to turn your daydreams, which are often pretty vague at this point, into specific, achievable goals.

Let's take the first of the two examples, "to make a lot more money." What's a lot more? After some reflection, you think along these lines: "I made $50,000 last year. If I can increase the business in my territory by 35 percent, I'll make $75,000. While that may seem like a lot, the economy has turned around and it is expanding. I have several new customers who are going to invest in major new equipment, and a few of my good customers are growing and expanding. If I work hard and smart, I might be able to do it."

Your earlier, vague goal of "making a lot more money" has now been turned into something very specific: "to make $75,000 in the new calendar year."

This is a key step in the process because the specific detail of the goal is part of what gives it power. If your goals are vague and abstract, they have less power to shape and direct your behavior.

You should now have a piece of paper with your specific, prioritized goals written on it. When you've reached that point, you're ready for the final step.

Step 6. Refine. Because of the power of a goal to direct your behavior, it's very important that you write your goals exactly as you want them to be. A great deal of your time and effort will be directed toward achieving those goals over the next year. It behooves you to make sure the goals are right. You wouldn't want to waste any of that time and energy.

Once you have created written, specific goals, take a moment to judge them by some standards. See if they measure up to the following questions. If so, good. If not, rewrite them to meet the criteria listed below.

1. **Are they specific?** Does each goal specify, in detail, exactly what you want to accomplish? Can you make it more specific than it already is?

2. **Are they measurable?** Can somebody else tell if you have achieved your goal? Have you stated it in measurable terms? Look at the example. "To make a lot more money" may be realistic, but it's not measurable. What's "a lot more"? By turning that phrase into a measurable unit, $75,000, you have made your goal measurable.

3. **Are they realistic?** Deciding to be elected president of the United States might be a worthwhile goal, but it might not be realistic for you. This is where your daydreams meet reality. Your goals should require a stretch and require you to work hard to accomplish them, but they shouldn't be so optimistic that you have no realistic chance of achieving them.

4. **Do they have a specific time frame?** Every goal should have a deadline for completion. That helps put power into it. A goal with no deadline has little motivational power. For each goal, specify the date by which the goal will be attained. In the example, the goal "To make $75,000 in the next calendar year" has a specific time frame. All the money has to be made by December 31st of next year.

5. **Are they worthwhile?** Is this a valuable goal that will be applauded by others when it is attained? Is it something that you'll be proud of? You might have a very specific, measurable, realistic, time-sensitive goal such as this: "To drink a case of beer four of every five evenings during the workweek, every week in the month of December." While that goal meets all the other criteria, it's not very worthwhile. Your goals should be worthwhile.

The refining step is the last step of the goal-setting process. By the time you have finished it, you will have a written set of goals that express your view of your ideal accomplishments in a powerful, motivational way.

Applying the Goal-Setting Process to Improve Your Sales Results

It's easy to see that you can apply the goal-setting process in an unlimited number of ways. You can apply it to specific, day-to-day activities, like creating goals for every one of your accounts, for example. What do you want to accomplish this year, or this month, in each account? When you answer this question, you've set a goal. On the other hand, you can apply the goal-setting process to more general, long-range issues, like your long-term financial, social, or spiritual progress.

In any case, setting goals is the first step in gaining control of your time and becoming proactive. The only question is where to begin.

Think back to the onion analogy from Chapter 7. This time, apply the concept of layers of depth in the onion to yourself. Figure 11-2 illustrates the application levels for goal setting.

You can create goals for yourself at each level of the onion. On the most superficial level are goals having to do with your sales calls and your accounts. Goals at this level are necessary for you to take control of your sales time and become a proactive salesperson. At the next level are goals for acquiring skills and sales techniques. This book, for example, should generate a great number of those kinds of goals. The next level consists of goals having to do with your attitudes and personal growth. Finally, at the deepest level, are goals having to do with your purpose in life and your reason for living. These are the deepest goals—spiritual issues—that affect every other goal above them.

FIGURE 11-2

Personal Growth from the Inside Out

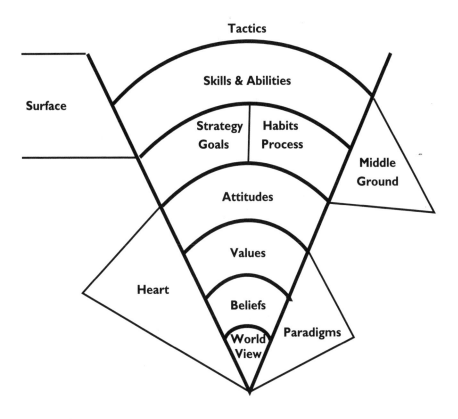

Here's a list, starting from the surface and working down, of the areas that I believe are worthy of your goal-setting efforts.

- Goals for every sales call.
- Goals for every A account.
- Annual sales, gross profit, and market share goals.
- Goals for the attainment of sales skills.
- Personal learning goals.

- Long-term goals for your career, finances, family, social, spiritual, and physical progress.
- An ultimate, purpose in life goal.

Where you start doesn't make much difference. I've found that you can begin at any level and move upward or downward as you feel inclined. Sooner or later, however, you should address all the levels.

Review your long-term and annual goals once a year. I believe that you ought to devote a day or so every year to nothing but this process. Review your A account and short-term goals monthly, and write new ones for the coming months. Review your weekly and daily goals each week and each day, and create goals for your sales calls every day.

This goal-setting discipline will put you on the track to focused, directed behavior. That is the first step for the salesperson who is becoming an Adept Human Resources Manager.

⚓ *You're always more effective when you focus on unleashing your strengths and managing your weaknesses.*

This is one of the principles that changed my life. As a younger man, much of my personal development efforts were focused on overcoming my weaknesses. I expended a lot of energy with little results. Then, as often happens to me, a comment someone made clicked in my brain, and I discovered the truth of this principle. I still recall the circumstances. It was a sermon by a minister in a Sunday morning worship service in a small church in Brighton, Michigan. I remember talking excitedly with him after the service. Of course! You'll always be more effective if you leverage your strengths, making the most of the talents and gifts you have, instead of trying to overcome your weaknesses.

You're probably familiar with the Pareto Principle, or the 80–20 law. We often apply it to our customers: Eighty percent of our sales come from twenty percent of our customers. You'll find that to be close to true almost all of the time. In fact, you can apply the Pareto Principle to almost any area of human endeavor and find it will hold true. So it shouldn't be surprising to find that it holds true about managing ourselves.

Eighty percent of our performance comes from twenty percent of our efforts. If we can discover the twenty percent that represents our strengths, and then learn to apply our energy to our strengths, we'll get far better results. The trick is to discover your strengths, and then to develop ways in which they can be brought to bear on your current position. Here's an example from my life.

I discovered, early in my professional career, that I had a gift for speaking. I actually enjoyed speaking to groups of all sizes, and I was good at it. In fact, given a choice between making a one-on-one presentation or speaking to a group, I'd prefer the group.

Once I came to realize the truth of this principle, I tried to find ways to bring my group presentation skills to bear on my sales career. Whenever I was scheduled to make a presentation, I'd try to arrange for several of my customers to be there, rather than just one. I developed small seminars to train my customers in the use of my products, so that I could speak to them in groups, not just individually. I'd arrange for lunch meetings at which I provided lunch and made presentations to small groups. I'd volunteer to speak at any gathering of my potential customers—trade shows, conferences, meetings etc. In all these ways I could bring my strengths in speaking to my sales job. As a result, I multiplied my effectiveness and realized great success as a salesperson. It's no surprise then, that today public speaking at conventions and national sales meetings is a major part of my practice.

Here's a process to use to implement this powerful principle.

Step 1. Assess your strengths. Who's the human resources manager for you? You are! So it's your responsibility to identify your unique set of strengths. Here are a couple of ways to do it.

1. Think about yourself objectively. Ask and answer these questions:
   a. What kinds of activities come very easily to you?
   b. What kinds of activities do you enjoy?
   c. What kinds of activities seem to get you the best results? As you answer these questions, you'll often find a pattern developing. That pattern can be a good indication of where your unique strengths lie.

2. Take a test. The science of assessment has progressed in leaps and bounds in the last couple of decades. Some seemingly simple assessments can be almost frightening in how much they can tell you about yourself. Taking an assessment or a battery of them can be one of the best things you do to reveal your own strengths and weaknesses.

Step 2. Get someone's validation or confirmation. While it is up to you to identify your strengths, don't trust your own judgment completely. Once you have an idea where your strengths lie, talk to someone who knows that part of you and get their input. Your manager should be a great source of this validation, as should your spouse or significant other.

Listen carefully to their input, and revise your opinion accordingly.

Step 3. Find ways to apply those strengths to your job. Now your creativity comes into play. The more you are able to creatively apply your strengths to your job, the easier your job will become and the more enjoyable it will be for you. There is no one formula for this part of the process because no combination of strengths and jobs is the same. You have to figure this one out on your own.

Recall the example of how I used my speaking ability in my sales positions. Now it's up to you to apply your strengths to your situation.

Time Management

One of the most important areas to manage effectively is the use of your time. This is a larger issue for professional salespeople than for people in many other types of jobs because your time is so much in your control. You know that you could, if you chose to, spend hours a day not working, and it would be some time before your company realized it. What is far more common than the salesperson who doesn't work, however, is the salesperson who spends hours not working *effectively*.

The difference between just working and working effectively is good time management. All this means that, if you're going to succeed in the Information Age, you must be more disciplined and smarter about using your time effectively than ever before.

Time management is a daily battle. You will never win the war. It's not like a big sale that once closed, you can look back at and see a definite end to. Time management doesn't generate a major feeling of accomplishment. There is no great victory. Instead, there is a daily struggle. Some days you win more battles than others, but every day you're in the contest.

On one hand, you have all the forces that strive to suck away your energy and time. If you're not careful, you can spend most days being totally reactive. While there is some satisfaction in being incredibly busy taking care of other people's problems and concerns, if you work reactively you only work everyone else's agenda while abandoning your own.

If you're going to be a successful Information Age salesperson, you need to work your own agenda. You need to take proactive control of your day and do the things that you know are the best things to do. That requires that you fight the battle for control of your time every day.

Ten Commandments for Good Sales Time Management

1. **Plan precisely for the use of your sales time.** "Sales time" refers to the time when you're face-to-face with your customers. It's the fundamental reason for your job. Think about it. There is someone in your company who can do everything else that you do. The one thing you do that no one else does is meet with your customers face-to-face. It's the defining moment of your job. It's the part of your job through which you bring value to your company.

   Unfortunately, it's very easy to go through the motions of each sales call without taking the time to plan. Most salespeople have only vague sales call plans, if any. From my own personal experience, as well as my experience with the literally thousands of salespeople I've trained, I've come to the conclusion that it only takes three minutes to plan a sales call. A daily investment of about 15 to 20 minutes will allow you to thoroughly plan for every sales call.

   The results for sales calls that begin with a plan will be far greater than for those that don't. Without a plan, it's just too easy to get sidetracked and reactive. When you're finished with the day, you feel exhausted from all the problems you solved and the tasks you completed, but you haven't caused the things to happen that you wanted to make happen. So you've spent your day being busy but ineffective. That's a luxury you can no longer afford.

   Planning for the most effective use of your sales time will both increase the quantity as well as improve the quality of face-to-face interactions with your customers. You can apply an abbreviated version of the planning process from Chapter 3 to the discipline of creating powerful sales call plans.

2. **Plan to make good use of uncontrollable downtime.** You know what uncontrollable downtime is: It's those times that occur without notice, when your day is turned upside down through no fault of your own.

    It's the time when you've driven an hour to keep an appointment with a client you've been wanting to see, who called in sick but nobody told you. All at once you're confronted with uncontrollable downtime. The first temptation is to waste that time. I learned about uncontrollable downtime the hard way.

    When I was selling surgical staplers, I often scrubbed with the surgeon who was learning to use the instruments. I was one of the people in caps, gloves, and mask, standing over the patient, across from the surgeon, in the operating room. When they were just learning to use the instruments, surgeons liked to have me there in case they had any problems with the staplers. Most of the surgical procedures in which the staplers were used were major bowel and gastric surgery, and those cases were usually scheduled first thing in the morning, generally at 7:00 a.m.

    I was working with a surgeon at a hospital about an hour's drive from my house. Because surgery started at 7:00 a.m., I needed to get to the hospital at about 6:30 a.m. so I could review the procedures and the instruments with the surgeon before scrubbing. That meant I had to leave my house around 5:00 a.m. I always made it a practice to bring a box of donuts for the operating room nurses, so I needed to leave at 4:30 a.m. to allow time to get to the donut shop. That meant getting up at 3:45 a.m.

    It's common practice to postpone major surgery if the patient has a fever. The surgical team never wants to add any stress to the patient if the patient has some kind of infection.

    You guessed it. Three days in row, as I stumbled into the OR suite at 6:30 a.m., having already been awake for about three hours, the OR Supervisor glanced at the surgical schedule, looked up at me, and said, "Oh, didn't anyone call you? Surgery has been postponed!"

On the third day, I decided the uncontrollable downtime was going to be an occupational hazard of my job and that, instead of becoming upset about it, I should take it in stride by being prepared for it.

Since then I have always carried some work with me wherever I go. That way, I'm not frustrated by uncontrollable downtime.

You need to do the same. In your briefcase, always have some literature about that new product to study, or that quote you need to price, or that paperwork to be completed. By being prepared, you're always ready to make good use of uncontrollable downtime.

3. **Prioritize your activities every day.** In a world that constantly bombards you with things to do, it's incredibly easy and extremely tempting to have your day shaped by the hundreds of demands and requests made by everybody else.

I call this the popcorn approach to your workday. Imagine a popcorn popper, the old kind with a hot plate on the bottom and a glass canister above it. Visualize the popcorn kernels lying in the bottom of the hot plate, vibrating in the sizzling oil. When it gets hot enough, one of the kernels explodes and careens off the side of the canister and drops back into the oil. A few seconds later another explodes and bounces off a different portion of the canister. Then another shoots off in a third direction, another in yet another direction, again and again. All that energy is dissipated as it shoots off in a countless number of directions.

That's an apt description of how some salespeople run their days. They are totally reactive to countless interruptions, their energy exploding in a thousand different directions. The only real way to take control of all these temptations and interruptions is to create a priority list every day and then stick to that list. That way you have a clear choice between working your agenda and working everyone else's.

If you have no priority list, then the choice is easy; it's always everyone else's agenda that takes precedence. At the end of each day, before you go home and join your family, take about ten minutes to create a list of everything you want to do tomorrow. Then go back and prioritize the items in order of importance. Which of all these items is the one that is likely to bring you the greatest result? After that, which is next? Number them in order of importance.

Tomorrow, when someone at the office wants you do something, realize that you have a choice. You can do what they want you to do or you can work on your agenda. Success belongs to the proactive salesperson, not the reactive one.

4. **Constantly evaluate the effectiveness of what you're doing.** As a straight-commission salesperson, I developed a couple of habits that have served me well over the years. One was the habit of asking myself, several times during the course of the day, this question: "Am I doing, right now, the thing that is the most effective thing for me to do?"

I can't tell you how many hundreds or thousands of times my answer was "No." Every time I answered myself in the negative, I had to change what I was doing and do the thing that was the most effective. That habit has not only served me well as a straight commission salesperson, but I find it to be one of the best time management tools as president of my own training and consulting business. My second habit was to *always do what's hottest first.* In other words, if I had two or more things to do, I'd always do the thing that was "hottest" first. What's hottest? Hottest is *closest to the money.* For example, if I had a choice between seeing one customer and closing the order, and seeing another to do a product demonstration, I'd close the order. That's closer to the money.

These two habits of daily time management are powerful weapons you can use in your daily battle.

5. **Cluster similar activities.** If you have ten phone calls to make, don't make two now, three later, and five this afternoon. Instead, make them all at one time. That way, the amount of time you spend transitioning to the next task will be significantly reduced.

6. **Create systems to handle routine tasks.** We all have routine things that we must do over and over again: fill out expense reports, create sales reports, complete other paperwork, file invoices, review back orders, etc.

You'll find that routine tasks can be handled very effectively if you create a system to handle them and then always use that system to complete the task. You only have to think about the best way to do some of these routine tasks once.

For example, if you have to fill out a weekly expense report, always put your receipts in the same portion of your brief-case. Always fill out your form at the same time of the week, in the same place. Again, the duplication of routine efforts makes them mindless tasks. Some things are best done mindlessly.

7. **Use an appropriate strategy for the size and potential of the account.** Some accounts need more attention than others. It doesn't take a rocket scientist to figure that out, but developing that concept into a workable daily routine is something else. Review the discussion of ABC ratings in Chapter 3. It means that some accounts should get a visit from you every six months and a phone call once a month. Others should get two visits a week.

Don't be afraid to use a phone or fax machine to keep in contact with your low-volume accounts. Invest your time in appropriate ways for the potential of each account you have. Do not treat everyone the same.

8. **Don't go into the office!** This is my number one negative rule. It's based on Kahle's law of office time. Kahle's law is an inviolate observation about nature that you can count on to the same extent that you count on the sun coming up every day. Kahle's law of office time is this: "If you plan on working in the office for 30 minutes, it will always take you two hours."

There is just something about going into the office that is inherently a time waster. People want to talk to you, you receive phone calls, there's mail to read, coffee to drink, and customer service people to chat with. Add that all up, and it's guaranteed to waste your time.

One of my clients once asked me about the design of a new office building she was erecting for her business. "What arrangements should I make for the salespeople?" she asked. "Should I build them each their own office, or should I invest in those modular office systems so that each one can have a workspace?"

I replied, "You should have one phone in a very crowded place. Make it as difficult for them to work in the office as possible. That way they won't come there!"

That's how strongly I believe in this law. Whatever you do, stay out of the office!

If you must go to the office, and I recognize that sometimes you must, then go in the last thing in the day, not the first thing in the morning. If you go in at 4:30 in the afternoon with a half hour's worth of work to do, you're much more likely to get it done in 30 minutes than if you attempt the same thing at 8 in the morning.

9. **Be conscious of time wasters, and work to eliminate them.** Time wasters are unconscious, time-wasting habits you have created over the years. You've become so accustomed to them that you're probably not even aware of them. The first step is to become conscious of them.

For years I had an unconscious time waster. Every time I experienced a bad call, one that didn't go the way I wanted it to, I had to find a coffee shop and buy myself a cup of coffee so that I could feel sorry for myself for 15 or 20 minutes. After that short pity party, I was ready to go back at it.

One day, I realized what I was doing: wasting all that time on a habit that didn't do me any good. I realized that self-pity was a luxury I couldn't afford. So I worked to eliminate that habit of drinking coffee and feeling sorry for myself.

I suspect that you may have created some unconscious habits that fall into the category of time wasters. Here's a list I've gathered from my seminars when I've asked participants to list some of their more cherished habitual time wasters. See if any of these sound familiar:

- Taking smoke breaks.
- Making personal calls.
- Running personal errands.
- Not making appointments, just showing up unexpectedly.
- Small talk with people in the office.
- Not planning your day.
- Reading the morning paper.
- Taking long lunches.
- Eating lunch by yourself instead of with a customer.
- Taking long coffee breaks.
- Being unorganized.
- Trying to do everything yourself instead of relying on your support people.

- Not trusting the system, double-checking everything.
- Hand delivering paperwork to the office instead of mailing it in.

Got the idea? You might have a special little time waster that you've treasured for years. If you're going to be effective in our time-compressed age, now is the time to work to eliminate it.

10. **Don't get caught up in immediate reaction.** Immediate reaction occurs when you have your day or a portion of a day planned, and then you receive a phone call or fax from one of your customers with a problem for you to solve. The natural tendency is to drop everything and work on the problem. After all, isn't that good customer service?

When you do that, you become reactive and you lose control of your day. Isn't there some way to provide service but stay in control?

The stumbling block is the assumption that just because someone calls, the problem is urgent and needs immediate attention. So you react immediately. But that isn't always necessary. Often, the situation isn't really urgent, and you can address it later.

All you need to do is ask this simple question of your customer: "Can I take care of it ... (fill in the most convenient time for you to do so)?" Often, your customer will say, "Sure, that's okay." On those occasions you will have regained control of your day, and you can proceed with your plan.

Granted, sometimes customers have urgent issues. On those occasions, you do need to take care of the problem as soon as you can. But if you ask the question, a good portion of the time you'll remain in control.

By asking the question, you refuse to get caught up in immediate reaction. Implement these ten commandments for good time management, and you'll make great strides in becoming an effective self-manager.

12

ADEPT HUMAN RESOURCES MANAGER: PART II

In chapter 11 we looked at the principles and processes you can use to direct your assets and energy into positive channels in order to leverage your strengths. No doubt, focusing on strengths and pursuing positive goals are powerful ways to unleash your potential.

Unfortunately, focusing on the positive is not the whole story. Even the most positive people occasionally get blindsided by adversity, hampered by depression, or frozen in fear. So there is another side to this hat. Not only is it important to unleash your strengths, it's also important to overcome negative influences. They are the events and influences that knock you off course and dissipate your energies. Fear, depression, adversity, and rejection are the negative forces that can sidetrack the most positive salespeople. To be an adept Human Resources Manager, you need to become effective at managing both positive and negative forces, which brings us to the first principle:

⚓ *You'll be more effective if you can eliminate the hindrances to your performance.*

Like so many of the principles, this one is also common sense applied to sales. The problem is not that salespeople don't agree with the validity of the principle; the problem is that they don't apply it.

Of course you'll be more effective if you can overcome the hindrances to your sales performance. We all have a memory of a call we didn't make because we were afraid of what we'd hear, or one that never happened because we told ourselves, "They won't buy, so why bother?" We all have had days when we've been too discouraged or depressed to give our best. And we've all had the experience of seeing some new technique or tactic, but not applying it because we were uncomfortable with it. These are all examples of being hindered by negative forces. Let's look at some of the most common.

Handling Failure and Adversity

Failure is probably the professional salesperson's most common experience. You probably make fewer than 50 percent of the appointments you attempt to make. You probably sell fewer than 50 percent of the proposals or demonstrations you make. You fail more often than you succeed. If you don't have a way to handle this continuous failure, you'll find that it can affect you emotionally, hindering your performance and maybe even driving you out of sales.

Dealing with failure is a skill that is rarely talked about, but absolutely essential to the success of a professional salesperson.

I certainly remember my failures more clearly than I do my successes. At one point in my sales career, I sold capital equipment, specifically, amplification equipment for classrooms for hearing-impaired children. The systems were sold to the special education school systems and were big-ticket, budgeted items.

In one year, there were twenty-nine deals available in my territory. Of those twenty-nine, I got twenty-eight orders. Ask me which one I remember most clearly and which one I learned the most from: You know it—my one failure.

Adversity is like failure in that it produces a negative situation for us. The difference is that adversity is not always our own doing. Failure is often a consequence of our own actions. It usually takes the form of the inability to achieve some objective or goal. When we fail, we don't achieve some positive thing for which we were striving. Adversity sometimes falls on us without any direct involvement of our part. It brings with it a negative situation— some pain that we weren't expecting. It hits all of us, not just professional salespeople. However, because salespeople live with failure and rejection so often, we are more susceptible to the negative consequences of adversity. It's easy to get depressed and down on ourselves when we fail if, at the same time, we're struggling with some kind of adversity.

One of my greatest challenges as a salesperson occurred after I decided to leave the amplification equipment company and accepted a position selling surgical staplers.

This was a major risk on my part. I was the number one salesperson in the nation for my former employer, with a good salary, a company car, and great prospects. However, I was bored and looking for another challenge. So I accepted a position that was the opposite in many ways. It paid straight commission, for example, with a draw that lasted only for the first six months. The salespeople bought their own demonstration samples and literature from the company. Before I accepted the offer, I calculated the amount of existing business in the territory. I felt that, if I could double the business within the first year, I'd be okay. After that, any increases would be real increases in my standard of living.

So I took the plunge and went off to New York for six weeks of intense training. While I was gone, the district sales managers changed, and I had a new boss. When I returned home from training, I was met by my new district sales manager, who announced that he had rearranged the territories. The territory for which I was hired wasn't exactly the territory I was going to receive. In fact, the territory I ended up with had only about 30 percent of the existing business I was depending on. My livelihood and the health and well-being of my family were in serious jeopardy.

I was outraged. How could they do this to me? What kind of company was this that would treat its employees that way? I immediately decided that I didn't want to work for them and began looking for a different job. However, it only took a few weeks of interviewing for me to realize that I was seen as unemployable. Most people with whom I interviewed viewed my quick desire to leave as a weakness in me, not in my company.

One thing led to another and, after six months, I owed the company $10,000 (a lot of money in the mid 1970s), my draw was finished, and I had few prospects for finding another job. Talk about being between a rock and a hard place!

That was adversity, compounded by my failure to sell the product effectively. How do you deal with failure and adversity? Here's a process that will work for you.

Step 1. Accept the new reality. No use moping about it. No use pretending that it'll go away or change or that it doesn't matter. It *does* matter or else you wouldn't be thinking about it. Accept that you failed. Accept that your situation is not what you'd like it to be.

Once you accept it and stop denying it or fighting it, you can go on from there.

At the same time that you accept the new reality, accept your responsibility to do something about it. No one is going to bail you out. The reality is that you're in this situation, and *you* need to do something about it.

When I was in the middle of the struggle with my failure under the new manager, I finally saw, in a moment of blinding clarity, that my situation was pretty much my own doing. It wasn't them, it was *me*! The realization of my personal responsibility took a great weight off my shoulders. If the problem was me, I could do something about it! I was once again in a situation where I could influence the world around me and affect my life. I was no longer a victim, depressed under the unjust weight of someone else's actions. Because the problem was in me, the power to solve it was also in me!

Step 2. Ask questions. This is a great time to learn. Remember, you'll generally learn more from your failures than you will from your successes, providing that you're ready and able to learn. One effective way to learn is to reflect on what happened and ask questions about it. How did it happen? Why? What did you do (or not do) to bring this situation about? What could you have done differently? How did your customer react? How did your competitor act? Is there some lesson in that?

Got the idea? Begin with questions.

In my situation, my question-asking routine led me to the conclusion that my own bitterness and negativity were the major problem. If I could do away with them, I could be more effective.

Step 3. Draw conclusions. Once you ask the questions, answer them fully. After each question you ask about the situation, follow it with this question that you ask about yourself: "What should I do differently in the future?"

If you ask, "What did I do to create this situation?" and your answer is, "I didn't thoroughly prepare my presentation," then ask the second question, "What should I do differently in the future?"

The answer to that question is your conclusion: "I should make sure I am thoroughly prepared for every presentation."

These conclusions, or reflections on your behavior, are the most important fruits of your failure. Almost any failure is worthwhile if it stimulates some changed behavior and deeper understanding on your part. It's not what happens that's important in the long run; it's what you learn from it that counts.

I began writing this book in the spring of 1998, as the Detroit Red Wings had just won their second Stanley Cup championship. Two sweeps of opponents, two years in a row. It was truly an exciting moment, made even more delectable by talks of the beginning of a winning dynasty. In the newspaper shortly after their victory was an interview with Darren McCarty, one of the Red Wings. Reflecting on the team's previous years of failure, he remarked, "You have to lose before you can win." He meant, of course, that losing (or failure), if you learn from it, is a necessary stepping-stone to success.

That's a powerful principle that's worth spotlighting:

⚓ *If you learn from them, failure and adversity are incredibly powerful steps toward success.*

In my situation, I concluded that I needed to stimulate myself to be positive and to overcome my bitterness and resentment with positive self-confidence.

Step 4. Play with situations. Play little "what if" games in your imagination. If you're in a miserable situation, begin by asking yourself questions like, "What if I did this ...?" or "What if I did that ...?"

See if doing that doesn't stimulate some creative and exciting possibilities for you. I asked myself how I could overcome my internal bitterness and resentment. I played the "what if" game and came up with a novel approach. I decided that I needed to change my attitudes. I was caught in a negative mode and I needed to change that to a positive mode. I reasoned that I needed to put positive, confident thoughts into my head. If I could fill my head with positive thoughts, I'd gradually be able to change my negative attitude.

At the time, I was living on the outskirts of my territory, and I had a daily 45-minute drive into the metropolitan Detroit area on

Interstate 96. I decided to make use of that 45 minutes every morning to put positive thoughts into my head.

I spent an evening finding all the powerful, positive promises in the Bible, and wrote them on 3- by 5-inch cards. Each morning, I'd hold the 3- by 5-inch cards in front of me on the steering wheel and flip through them over and over, reading them repeatedly as I drove into the city. As I bathed my mind in positive, confident ideas, I slowly changed my attitude and began to turn my bitterness and resentment into optimism.

Step 5. Focus on short-term possibilities. When life seems to have dealt you the most unfair blow and the future looks miserable, stop contemplating the future. It's no fun thinking about how miserable you're going to be. Instead, focus on the short-term possibilities.

I'm a great believer in long-term goals. But I also have been through enough miserable situations in my life to know that there are times when it's best to forget (for now) those long-term goals and focus on the positive things you can do *today*!

I cannot tell you how many times in my life I've found this discipline to be a powerful tonic to a depressed view of the future. Instead of thinking about next year, think about tomorrow. What positive things can you do tomorrow, or better yet, today? What's the single most positive thing you can do today? Give yourself realistic, short-term goals. I mean really short-term—today and tomorrow. Think in terms of positive actions. You might not be able to create any long-term or mid-term goals in your current state of mind, but you still have the ability to select right from wrong, good from bad, and positive from negative. So focus on the very short term. Do the most positive things you can think of to do today, and don't worry about long-term goals.

In my example situation, with no draw, no commissions, no salary, and lots of financial responsibilities, I couldn't think in terms of my long-term financial goals. I decided to focus on today and tomorrow, and do the best things I could do in the short term. Instead of thinking about developing an account next month, I'd visit it today. I discovered a discipline I turned into a habit that was to serve me well from then on. Several times during the course of the day, I'd ask myself, "Am I doing the thing that is the single most effective thing for me to be doing right now?" If the answer was "no," I changed what I was doing.

At the same time, I remember deciding that, outside of my working day, the single most positive thing I could do was exercise. It always made me feel better. I knew it to be a good thing. So I began an exercise program.

Were these two things strategically designed to meet some long-term goal of mine? No! Were they my best response for the need to do something positive every day? You bet!

In neither case was I focused on long-term goals. However, I wasn't in the kind of circumstance where I felt long-term goals were possible. I couldn't see how I was going to survive my current mess. So I focused on the very short-term, positive things I could do today. When I was squarely in the middle between the rock and the hard place trying to sell surgical staplers, I couldn't imagine paying off that $10,000 debt. So I didn't think about it. Instead, I focused on using each day in the most positive way I could.

Step 6. Act. Sooner or later, you've got to do something. There is something about action that begets more action. If you can't figure out what to do and you're caught in a confused mental or emotional paralysis, force yourself to *do something*. It really doesn't matter what you do, as long as you start doing. Once you get moving, you'll find it easier to move in positive and thoughtful ways.

I've found that when I'm in the middle of a funk brought on by miserable circumstances or my own failure, I become paralyzed by my own thoughts. One of the most helpful things to do is to do something. Act! Stop thinking and do something! Action begets action. Start moving and you'll quickly feel like moving some more.

Oh yes, in case you're wondering, in six months I was able to pay off the debt, and I began making more money than I had imagined possible. What was an absolutely hopeless and miserable situation changed into one of the most financially rewarding, satisfying experiences of my life.

Surviving the Tidal Wave
of Information

A new threat is bearing down on salespeople. Here's the issue: Because of the rapid explosion in the quantity of information sloshing around us, it's easy to be overwhelmed and rendered ineffective by the sheer amount of it. Think of how many product brochures you need to review every year, how many memos from the higher-ups, how many reports of various types, pricing information, service bulletins—and that's just on the internal side of the business. Then factor in the amount of information being generated by your customers—their needs and interests, the names and situations of each of the key contacts, their changing product lines, concerns, and competitors. Now stir in the process information, the tools and procedures you use to do your job—the new computer program, forms, phone numbers, fax sheets, form letters, E-mail messages, and Internet information. Finally, pour in the marginal information that can be enticing yet not very productive—the 102 TV stations we can now get on digital cable, the slew of unsolicited E-mail messages, the growing pile of bulk mail enticements, the 40,000-plus new books published in the U.S. alone each year, and the new publications and newsletters in whatever format.

All these pieces of information are hardly droplets by themselves. But when added together and dumped on you in the typical week, they can form a tidal wave of information, washing you away under their sheer quantity and rendering you ineffective. When I teach my module on information management to salespeople at my seminars, I often ask them if they could spend at least eight hours a week doing nothing but considering all the information that comes their way each week. The resulting show of hands is often unanimous. Think of it, at least eight hours a week doing nothing but dealing with the tidal wave of information. That's 20 percent of the workweek. And that's minimal. That brings us to our next principle:

⚓ **The quantity of information that comes your way can render you ineffective.**

If you're going to become a skillful practitioner of the fifth hat, then you need to be adept at information management. In Chapter 3 we discussed the issue of information management from the perspective of collecting and using good information in order to enable you to make good decision and create effective plans. In this chapter, we discuss information management from the perspective of gaining control of the amount of information so that you will not be rendered ineffective.

THE INFORMATION MANAGEMENT PROCESS

Step 1. Develop some criteria for screening most of the information that comes to you. Look at Figure 12-1.

FIGURE 12-1

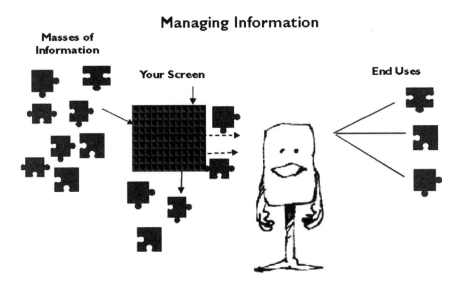

Because of the great quantity of information coming at you, you need a device to filter some of it out so that you never spend more then a few seconds looking at it. It's like a screen in the window on your house. It lets some things through, but also keeps a lot of undesirable things out. When it comes to information, you have a similar situation. You want to protect yourself with a screen around you that allows some information through but also keeps a lot of undesirable details out. There are a number of possibilities. You can use software to screen out some E-mail messages, voice mail to screen out phone calls, a good secretary or assistant to screen out people wanting to see you, and so on. You'll have to develop your own screen based on your situation.

At some point, however, you'll need to personally apply a screen to the incoming information. That screen should be the concept of "useful." In other words, every piece of information that comes at you ought to first be pressed through the filter of the question, "Is this likely to be useful to me?" If the answer is "No; it may be interesting, it may be entertaining, but it probably won't be useful," then don't spend any more time with it. Get rid of it immediately. If the answer is "Yes, this is likely to be useful," then consider it further.

Let's say you've arrived at the office and emptied your mailbox. There's a memo from the boss regarding a sales meeting coming up. That's useful. There's a new report showing the number of units you sold of some product this year versus the number sold last year. You use the screen of "useful," decide that it's not likely to make any difference to you, and toss it. There's a series of price increases for products you rarely sell. You decide the time it takes to study and file those isn't worth it, and toss those. There's an article written by one of your customers that was published in a trade journal. Your boss has made a photocopy for you. You decide this might be useful to read. There are four messages that people have called. Two are from customers, so you set those aside to answer. The third is from a credit card company with a new credit card to offer you. You toss that. The fourth is from one of the other salespeople in your company. You decide to return that call. And so on.

Applying the screening question, "Is this likely to be useful?" to every piece of information and demand for your time allows you to eliminate much of it right away, and thus protect a portion of your time from the tidal wave of information that presses on you daily.

Step 2. Determine the end uses of the information you consider. Now consider the information that's left. If it's useful, where are you going to use it? Let's think of all the possibilities. You'll certainly want information about your customers, so why not develop a set of customer files? Set up one manila folder for each A and B customer, and perhaps one for all of your C customers. Then, perhaps, an electronic duplicate of that file system in which to keep electronic information.

You'll also want information about your competitors. Develop an electronic and hard copy file for each of your major competitors.

You'll want information about the products and services you represent. Setting up files for each of those is appropriate.

You'll want information about the processes you use to bring together your products with your customers. Those files would include information about how to use the computer system, the reports and forms your company uses, etc. As a subset of those, you'll want files for good ideas about your own personal development—those behaviors and skills that you want to improve or add to your repertoire.

Now, when you look at the pile of stuff in your mailbox or all those E-mail messages on your screen, you'll look at them with a new perspective. Consider each piece that has made it through the initial screening. Where or how will you use it? File it in the appropriate place.

What if something doesn't fit into one of these prearranged files? You've got to question your initial judgment. If you can't think where it would be useful, perhaps it isn't useful and should be discarded.

Once you have your information appropriately arranged according to its end use, you're ready for step three.

Step 3. Handle the information. In other words, use it. Remember, if it's useful, you should be able to use it. So, what are you going to do with it? Take the memo from the boss as an example. You read the memo, make some notes in your day-timer or computer, and then toss the memo. You acted on it. You used it.

The article written by one of your customers first went into that customer's folder. Then, as you prepare for your next sales call, you review the article and decide to compliment the customer on it. You might even highlight a few passages to talk about. File that with the materials for your next sales call, and prepare to use it then.

You'll find that some information is worth studying, some should be filed and acted on at a later date, and some should be acted on immediately. Discipline yourself to implement this process, and you'll find yourself staying afloat in the tidal wave of information.

Dealing with Fear

One of the biggest obstacles to the success of any salesperson, your-self included, is fear. Fear reveals itself in a number of ways, any of which can sap your energy and diminish your success.

First is the fear of rejection, often said to be a salesperson's single biggest obstacle.

It's the fear of rejection that keeps you from calling on new accounts or meeting new people within your current accounts. We are all, at some level, afraid that we'll be turned down, and we don't like that feeling.

I recall my first professional sales call. I had to demonstrate a speech therapy instrument to a speech pathologist with a doctor-ate in the field. I had never demonstrated anything to anyone before. I was so scared and nervous that my hands were shaking. On top of everything, my district manager was with me, observing my performance! After the call, he asked me if I was aware that I was clenching and unclenching my fist over and over. Evidently, I was so tense that I was not conscious of my actions. That's fear.

Second is the fear of stretching yourself into areas beyond your comfort zone. This may be the experienced, professional salesper-son's most common fear. You have worked hard to create a large group of people who know you, generally like you, and are willing to spend time with you. They are your customers. You have a set of products or services with which you've grown very comfortable. More importantly, you have created a number of habits—ways in which you go about your job—that have generally been successful for you.

Because it's taken you some time to get to this point, you're naturally hesitant to do anything to jeopardize the status quo. That means that it's difficult to push beyond the comfortable dis-cussions you're accustomed to having. You're a little afraid to try some of the principles and processes I have discussed in earlier chapters of this book.

This fear keeps you in a rut—stuck in the performance levels you've become used to, stuck in the behavior patterns that have become comfortable for you. For most salespeople, it's not the fear of big things that is the issue; it's the fear of a thousand small things, all related to jeopardizing your fragile hold on your cus-tomers and your status quo.

It may be that none of these issues affects you. If that is the case, great; move on to the next chapter. But if you've ever been afraid to try something new in your job, afraid to be held accountable for some level of performance, afraid to stretch outside of your comfort zone, then you need to know how to deal with that fear.

Here's a process to help you overcome fear and successfully stretch yourself to new levels of productive behavior.

Step 1. Identify the issue. The first step in overcoming fear is to recognize that it is fear that is hindering you. I can remember more than a few miserable hours I weathered sitting at a desk trying to work up the courage to make cold calls. What stopped me was my fear of rejection. It took several hours of mental games before I realized that fear was the issue. I was afraid.

Until I realized that fear was the problem, I was powerless to overcome it. When you find yourself hesitant to do something—particularly if that thing is something new—ask yourself if the real issue isn't that you're afraid.

If you find yourself hesitant to meet new people, present a new product line, or try a new selling tactic, look inward to see where that hesitancy is coming from. If it's fear, acknowledge it and move forward.

Step 2. Look for deeper causes. Once you've decided that fear is the problem, think about *why* you might be afraid. Have you had a bad experience in the past? Is this something like a similar experience?

Then, argue with yourself. For example, if you discover you're afraid because of a bad past experience, tell yourself that was only one experience, and now you're older and wiser.

The process of arguing with yourself can provide logical support for you to attack your own fear. You can literally talk yourself out of your fear by reasoning with yourself.

Step 3. Remind yourself of past successes. If arguing with yourself doesn't work, remind yourself of a past success you've achieved by doing the thing that you now fear. I finally overcame my fear of cold calling by putting a picture of one of my best cus-

tomers—a customer I had acquired initially via a cold call—next to the phone. When I felt hesitant to make those cold calls, I'd pull the picture out and remind myself of my past success in dealing with that fear.

Step 4. Remind yourself of future rewards. What will happen if you are successful at doing the thing you fear? Will you earn more money? Acquire new customers? Provide yourself with a strategic advantage? If so, remind yourself of the result that you want. You can even put an illustration or picture of it near the phone or in your car where you can be reminded of your goal. Often, that visual reminder of your future rewards will be enough to stimulate you to action.

Step 5. Remind yourself of past rewards. Have you been successful in the past? Have you enjoyed the rewards of that success? Then remind yourself of some of your past rewards when you find yourself hesitant to do something.

Step 6. Act! Act! Act! Regardless of which of these techniques work for you, the important thing to do is *act*. Sooner or later, you must do something. Until you turn your thoughts into action, you haven't been successful. Ultimately, the only way to overcome fear is to act. All the other things I've talked about are only means to an end. They are self-management tools you can use to bring yourself to the point at which you can act. *Action* is the final victory over fear.

Dealing with Adversity:
Learned Optimism

In 1992, Dr. Martin Seligman published *Learned Optimism*, a book that may become one of the most significant books of the decade. In it, he describes his lifework. As a research psychologist, Dr. Seligman began by studying helplessness in dogs. In an early experiment, he put dogs into a cage from which they could not escape, and subjected them to mild shocks. After some effort at escape, the dogs would give up trying and lie down. Later, he put them into a cage from which they could easily escape, and subjected them to the same mild shocks. The dogs would just lie down and give up. Surprisingly, they did not attempt to remove themselves from the irritant. They had learned helplessness and hopelessness.

In subsequent experiments, Dr. Seligman found similar behavior in human beings. Put into a room and subjected to irritating noises from which they could not escape, they soon learned to give up. When put into a room with a mechanism that would turn off the noise, they still didn't try. They had learned helplessness and hopelessness.

From this beginning, Dr. Seligman continued to formulate a thesis he calls "learned optimism." It says, basically, that human beings learn to have either a pessimistic or an optimistic outlook. Dr. Seligman's book contains a self-assessment to measure the degree of pessimism or optimism of the reader.

Dr. Seligman's thesis arises from the way people explain negative events to themselves. When something negative happens, as it eventually will, the way you explain it to yourself determines your pessimistic or optimistic attitude. There are three components of this "explanatory style."

The first component is the degree to which you believe the event to be *permanent*. Pessimists believe negative events will be permanent, while optimists believe that they will be temporary. The second component is *pervasiveness*. Pessimists believe the causes of negative events are universal, affecting everything they do. Optimists believe them to be specific, and limited to the individual circumstances. The third component is *personal*. Pessimists believe that negative events are caused by themselves. Optimists believe that the world is at fault.

Here's how this behavioral perspective works in the everyday life of a salesperson. Let's say you visit one of your large accounts, and your main contact announces that the vice president for operations has signed a prime vendor agreement with your largest competitor, and that all of your business will be moved to that competitor within the next 30 days. *That's* a negative event.

As you drive away from the account, you think to yourself, "I blew it here. I should have seen it coming. I'm never going to learn this job. I'll blow the next one too. I mismanage them all."

Now, that's a pessimistic explanation of the event. Notice that you have explained it in a way that is personal: "*I* blew it." Your explanation is also permanent: "I'm *never* going to learn to do this job." And it's pervasive: "I mismanage them *all*."

Now stop a minute and analyze how you feel as a result of this explanation. You probably feel defeated, dejected, depressed, and passive. These are not the kinds of feelings that will energize you to make your next sales call.

Let's revisit the situation, this time offering optimistic explanations. The same event occurs—you receive bad news from your best account. As you drive away, you think to yourself, "They really made a bad mistake this time. It's a good thing the contract is only for a year. That gives me time to work to get it back. I'm glad it was only this account and no others."

That's an optimistic explanation because your explanations were not personal, permanent, or pervasive. How do you feel about your future as a result of this explanation? You probably feel energized and hopeful.

The event was the same in both examples. The only difference was the way you explained it to yourself. One set of explanations was optimistic, leading to energy and hope, while the other was pessimistic, leading to dejection and passivity.

Dr. Seligman has isolated optimistic behavior as one of the characteristics of successful people. Using various techniques he's developed, he predicted elections by analyzing each candidate's explanatory style. The most optimistic candidates often win the elections.

The implications for you are awesome. If you can improve your explanatory style and make it more optimistic, you'll create more positive energy and hope for yourself, no matter how difficult or negative the circumstances you must deal with.

Learned optimism can be one of your most powerful self-management techniques. It's based on this powerful principle:

⚓ **Your thoughts influence your feelings and your actions, and you can choose your thoughts.**

Here's the process Dr. Seligman recommends.

Step 1. Analyze your explanatory habits. Wait until you must deal with a negative event or an adversity in your life. Then, stop

and observe what you are telling yourself about the event. What do you believe about yourself and the reason why bad things happen? In Chapter 14 we'll discuss the issue of worldviews and your personal mission. That discussion will help put this in perspective For now, ask to what degree your explanations are personal, permanent, or pervasive.

Step 2. Note the consequences of your explanatory style. Pessimistic explanations always lead to passivity and dejection. Optimistic explanations always lead to energy and hope. Which is more likely to propel you to future success?

Step 3. If you're pessimistic, you must change the way you think. Your future success, your ability to achieve all your goals depends on your ability to rise up and meet adversity with renewed energy and optimism. You can do this by choosing to think differently.

Dr. Seligman makes the following suggestions.

1. *Distract your thoughts.* In other words, when you find yourself thinking negative and pessimistic thoughts, tell yourself to "Stop!" You can even say it out loud, or shout it to yourself. Just "Stop" thinking those things. Then, shift your thoughts to something else. I'd suggest you think about something that brings you pleasure or satisfaction, or something that you're good at.

2. *Dispute your explanations.* This is a longer-lasting approach. Argue with yourself. Reason your way out of your negative thoughts. Look at the evidence, or suggest alternatives. Reason from the implications or usefulness of what you're thinking.

In our example, on the way to your car after your miserable sales call, you are thinking to yourself, "I blew it here. I should have seen it coming. I'm never going to learn this job. I'll blow the next one, too. I mismanage them all."

When you catch yourself thinking defeating thoughts, argue with yourself. Think, "Wait a minute. While it's true I may have been able to do something if I had seen this coming, the truth is that the VP would never see me. The other company must have had some special 'in.' That doesn't mean that this will happen anywhere else. It's just this account. There certainly isn't any evidence of this happening anywhere else. And the truth is that the entire purchasing department is not happy about this course of events. If I stay close to the account, they may find lots of reasons to continue to do business with me."

What you've done is argue with yourself in order to change your thought processes. As a result of thinking differently, you have more energy, more hope, and therefore more likelihood of success in the future.

You can change your thoughts. You can choose to think differently. You can choose to believe differently. That fundamental decision about how you think can affect your future success more than any other single decision.

Through his scientific research, Dr. Seligman has discovered a truth that has been known for thousands of years. The apostle Paul, writing in the book of Romans, counseled new Christians to "Be transformed by the renewing of your mind." Solomon said, "As a man thinks in his heart, so is he." Your choice of what to think about, and how to think about what happens to you, is one of the most important choices you'll ever make.

If you're going to become a master of the fifth hat, choose your thoughts wisely.

Trying on the Fifth Hat

I know, you're overwhelmed. I would be too. The Adept Human Resources Manager's hat contains more principles and processes than any other, and no wonder. You're an incredibly complex, potentially powerful entity. Managing yourself in order to wring the most value from your strengths and abilities is a complex, never-ending challenge. Let's start by reviewing the principles:

1. *You are always more effective when you set goals.*
2. *You're always more effective when you focus on unleashing your strengths and managing your weaknesses.*
3. *You'll be more effective if you can eliminate the hindrances to your performance.*
4. *If you learn from them, failure and adversity are incredibly powerful steps toward success.*

5. *The quantity of information that comes your way can render you ineffective.*

6. *Your thoughts influence your feelings and your actions, and you can choose your thoughts.*

That's a lot to incorporate into your life, but you do have some very effective processes to assist you with the task. They include processes designed for:

- Goal setting
- Unleashing strengths
- Dealing with fear
- Handling failure and adversity
- Information management
- Learned optimism

How do you work all this into your life?

Reflecting on my experience, I'd suggest you start with identifying your strengths. I recall that insight being such a powerful turning point in my life that I expect it may have the same impact on you. So begin there, and build some energy and momentum from the realizations and successes that process generates.

You can't really decide to implement the processes for handling adversity and failure until you find yourself in those situations. Don't be impatient. You'll be suffering from one or the other soon enough. Keep this book as a reference, remembering that there is some insight to help you when those negative forces descend on you.

Until then, keep the focus positive. Set goals. Go all the way back to the first hat, Astute Planner, and review the suggestions in the section titled "Trying on the First Hat." Each of those planning sessions presents opportunities to set goals.

When you have uncovered your strengths and set goals, you'll find yourself moving along in a powerful and positive pattern. Add the other processes as you have time and occasion. That will give you a good start toward implementing the fifth hat.

Wearing the Fifth Hat

Confident. Self-assured. Those are powerful characteristics. That's how you'll feel when you begin to gain the competencies of the fifth hat. You'll have the knowledge that you're working in the most effective ways you can, that you're using the strengths and gifts your creator gave you, that you know how to survive the difficult days of a salesperson's life.

Most of all, you'll have the knowledge and assurance that come from experience, that you're gaining mastery of the greatest obstacle a salesperson faces—yourself!

APPLICATION: USING THE SIX HATS TO TURN CHALLENGES INTO OPPORTUNITIES

Challenge: I have so much paperwork and other things to do that I don't have enough time to sell.

This is an issue that can render you ineffective and sidetrack your career. Generally speaking, your company pays you to bring money into the organization, either by acquiring new customers or by expanding the business with current customers. If you spend your time doing other things, you're jeopardizing the value you bring to your company.

It may be that your job description includes other duties in addition to selling. In my experience, that situation almost always leads to less and less time spent selling, and more time spent doing the operational side of your job. That's because it's always much easier to react to the operational tasks that present themselves than it is to proactively create activity on the sales side. The "other stuff" invariably expands and pushes the sales efforts out of your day. It's so common, in fact, that I have an acronym for it: the dreaded OSE (other stuff expansion). If you're in a hybrid job, part sales and part operations, you are particularly susceptible to OSE.

Even if you are not in a hybrid position, as a salesperson you are still vulnerable to OSE. There are reports to read, memos to peruse, new sell sheets to study, invoices to file, notes to rewrite, inside people to converse with, other salespeople to ruminate with—the list of OS goes on and on. With the incredible expansion of information that marks the Information Age, you're vulnerable to being rendered ineffective by the sheer mass of *stuff.*

APPLYING THE SIX HATS

This is an example of the kind of real-life problem that has a serious impact on the day-to-day life of a salesperson. It's not the kind of thing you are taught in a sales training class, but it does significantly impact your performance and your career.

There are three possible responses to this challenge. First, you can do nothing and continue to work your job in the same way you have been. As long as you're meeting your goals and your company is happy with your performance, there may be no reason to change. But for most salespeople, one of the two parties—you or your company—is becoming unhappy. Some change must occur or you'll find yourself in a situation you don't want to be in.

The second and third responses are that your company changes its expectations of you, or you change the way you're doing your job. Let's work on the first possibility.

Put on your fourth hat (Skillful Influencer), but this time focus your skills on your company, not your customers. Treat your company like a customer. Identify the power structures and political connections inside your organization. Spend some time with your manager and other key people trying to understand their SPOO and PIE as they relate to your job description. Then carefully prepare your case for a redefinition of your job, just as you'd prepare a major presentation for a customer. Make that presentation using the principles and processes outlined in Chapters 9 and 10. If this effort is successful, you'll be able to influence your company to change.

Unfortunately, it doesn't always work that way. Your company, for a variety of reasons, might decide not to change. In that case, *you* are the party who must change. This is the time to exercise discipline and stick to some of the time management processes outlined in Chapter 11. Exercise your skills as an Adept Human Resources Manager, making sure that you're managing your greatest asset—yourself.

Begin by staying out of the office as much as possible. If you must go into the office, go at the very latest point that you can in the course of the day. In other words, don't go there first thing in the morning; rather, go at the end of the day. That will free up some of your selling time. Remember the rule of OSE (other stuff expansion). If you go into the office the first thing in the morning, you'll suffer OSE and not get out to the selling side of your job until way past when you thought you'd be at it.

Use your goal-setting process to set specific goals for the selling side of your job, and spend a lot of time planning and preparing for each day. If you don't proactively attack that portion of the day devoted to selling, the reactive portion devoted to other stuff will invariable push out selling time. You'll need to be even more disciplined about planning and preparing.

Cultivate relationships with the support staff in your company, and try to download as much of your nonselling stuff to them as possible. They can return some calls, check on the status of orders, mail out samples and literature, and solve customer problems. The list of things your company's support staff could do for you is limited only by your imagination.

In all of this, your disciplined application of the principles and processes of the fifth hat will be crucial. The key word here is *disciplined*. It means that every day you're going to have to fight the battle for the effective use of your time. Discipline yourself to practice these processes daily. Should you let down your discipline and relax, OSE will roar back with a vengeance and render that day ineffective.

You know what to do and you know how to do it. The key to long-term victory over OSE is your disciplined implementation.

13
THE SIXTH HAT: MASTER LEARNER

The sixth hat is my favorite. It's the fundamental, foundational hat. The competencies related to it provide the support for all the other hats. Without mastering this hat, you'll find it very difficult to master the others.

Picture a tree (Figure 13-1).

FIGURE 13-1

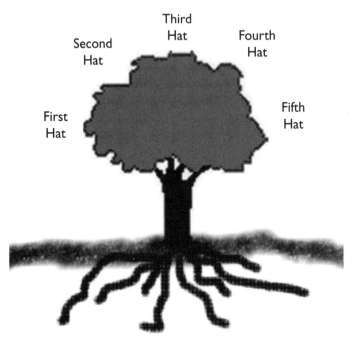

Second Hat

Third Hat

Fourth Hat

First Hat

Fifth Hat

Sixth Hat—Learning

The roots are hidden beneath the surface. The trunk, branches, and leaves are the parts we see. Yet the roots are what bring support and sustenance to all the other parts.

So it is with the sixth hat. These are the competencies that lie beneath the surface, that support and sustain all the others. With the sixth hat competencies, the other, more visible, competencies will constantly grow and thrive, providing you with a lifetime of personal and career success. Without the sixth hat, you'll eventually wither under the onslaught of a turbulent environment.

Remember the discussion of turbulent times in Chapter 1? Let's revisit it for a moment. We observed that we live in times that are changing at a more rapid pace than at any time in the history of the human race.

It's my belief that the only sustainable, effective response to a rapidly changing world is cultivating the ability to change ourselves. The first five hats provide direction, structure, and focus in your quest to change yourself. Together, they describe a powerful and effective approach to the changing situations that you and other salespeople face. When the need is to change and grow, they show you the branches and twigs on which that growth should take place.

But the task before you can be overwhelming. Up to this point, we've discussed dozens of principles and processes. You can't possibly implement all of them instantly. How do you sort them out? How do you prioritize, focus, and begin the process of implementing the hats? How do you gain the competencies that we've discussed? How do you do that in a way that reflects the speed demanded by our changing world? How do you master a hat in a few months rather than a few years?

It's one thing to understand the concepts, principles, and processes of the Six Hats, but it's another to actually act on them. The underlying question is, "How do you make the Six Hats a part of your daily routine?" The answer is that you've got to learn.

I know that sounds trite, but it isn't. Learning—especially learning to learn—is the greatest of all the hats. It's the root system for all the growth that takes place above it. If you're going to become a master of the Six Hats, you must change your behavior so that you are acting with knowledge of the Six-Hat principles and implementing the Six-Hat processes.

The underlying issue, the core problem for you, is to learn quickly and effectively. The word *learn* might be giving you some problems. When we hear the word *learning* it often brings back images of our days in high school or college, sitting in classes and absorbing sometimes irrelevant information. That's one definition of learning, but it's not what I'm talking about. In the Information Age, the only really useful learning is learning that results in changed behavior. In other words, if you think you've learned something but you haven't changed the way you act, you haven't really learned. Learning is synonymous with changed behavior.

Here's my definition. Think of it as the primary principle behind the sixth hat:

⚓ *Learning is the process of taking in new information or developing new insights, and then changing your behavior in positive ways as a result.*

"Continuous personal growth," "continuous improvement," and "rapid development" are other, equally accurate terms. The problem for many of us is that we never really learned how to learn. We learned how to earn grades in school, but I'm talking about real life now, not academics. Academics is primarily concerned with what goes on in your head. I am primarily concerned with how you act. We all know there is often no real connection between academic learning and real-life effectiveness. I'm sure every reader of this book knows someone who was a good student academically, but less than successful in real life.

I'm sure some of you are thinking, "But I can learn. Look, I've gotten this far. Isn't that an indication of my ability to learn?" Sure it is, but do you know how to learn as quickly and effectively as you need to in order to be successful in a world that is moving much faster than it did just a few years ago?

Learning is like playing golf. Now, I can play golf. I know this because I've done it two or three times. Every time I've played golf, I've gotten the ball into the hole. That's the idea of the game, right? But you know and I know that I don't golf well. For me to golf well, I'd need to invest some time and money into learning to be competent at the sport. I'd need to take some lessons from a competent coach and learn the principles and processes involved in a good golf swing. I'd need to acquire some good tools (clubs, shoes, etc.), and then I'd need to discipline myself to practice and continuously improve. After I'd done all of that, my golfing skills would inevitably improve.

Similarly, you can learn, but can you learn as well as you could? Just as you could dramatically improve your golf game if your livelihood depended on it, you can dramatically improve your learning competency—and your livelihood *does* depend on it. If you don't become good at learning, you won't become good at the competencies of any of the other hats. Learning is the fundamental skill that enables you to acquire the competencies symbolized by the other hats.

To get better at learning, just like golf, you need to invest time and money in it; you need to have a competent coach to work with you; you need to understand the key principles and processes; you need to acquire effective tools; and you need to discipline yourself to practice until you achieve a greater level of competency.

Let's start with a principle:

⚓ Learning is your primary responsibility.

One of the most common complaints I hear from salespeople goes something like this: "My company never really trained me to do this." I can understand that sentiment. In my experience (although as a sales trainer, I have a prejudiced perspective), very few companies do a decent job of training their salespeople. That's too bad. They would be much better off if they did spend time and money training and retraining their salespeople. But, that's not the whole story.

When I hear that complaint about training, I often answer, "So what?" So what that your company never trained you well? So what that they didn't spend lots of time and money on you? So what? Learning, growing, and continuously improving are *your* responsibility. If you're not performing as well as you could, it's not their fault, it's yours! Remember my experience with the new manager in the surgical stapler company? I kept sinking deeper and deeper into financial and emotional muck, until it dawned on me that it wasn't them, it was me! It was *my responsibility* to be successful. It was my job to learn what I needed to learn to do the job well. It was totally up to me!

When I had that great insight, it changed my attitude and my performance for the rest of my life. Once I accepted responsibility for my own actions, I realized that I could learn how to be successful. As long as I remained, in my mind, a victim of my company's omissions, I'd wallow forever in self-pity and helplessness. When I realized it was me, not them, I was suddenly energized with the knowledge that I could change.

What a powerful truth! Learning, changing, growing, continuously improving—they are your responsibility. Becoming a Six-Hat Salesperson—that's your responsibility. Your company may train you, but it's still your responsibility to apply that training. When you realize the truth that it is your responsibility, an amazing future becomes possible.

You can learn, and if you can learn efficiently and effectively, you can change, you can grow, and you can succeed at whatever level you select. There's hope and optimism in every situation, because you can learn.

Not only is it your responsibility to learn, but it's your *primary responsibility*. As a Six-Hat Salesperson, the one thing you will continue to do until you retire is learn. That competency supports and nourishes every twig and leaf of your job. You'll need, for example, to continuously learn new products and services. Your company will develop them more rapidly than in the past. You'll have to understand them more rapidly than in the past, and use that understanding to persuasively communicate to your customers.

You'll need to continuously learn about the people you encounter along the way—customers, bosses, support staff, and so on. They'll change in at least two ways. The individuals themselves are likely to turn over more rapidly than in the past, so you'll have to continually meet and relate to new people. And as individuals, they will continually change and grow. Their jobs will change, their interests and needs will change, and you'll have to adjust accordingly.

You'll need to continuously learn about the problems and opportunities your customers encounter, the applications for your products and services, and the principles and processes to put all of those together in a way that is effective for your customers, satisfying for you, and profitable for your company.

When you accept and internalize the truth in this principle, you're well on your way to mastering the sixth hat.

⚓ *In order to become good at learning, you must invest in it.*

If you're shivering in the middle of a cold winter day and you want to get some warmth from the fireplace, you don't expect to get the heat first, and then put in the firewood. You've got to first invest time and money in acquiring the firewood, preparing the fire, and lighting it. Then you get heat as a result. Likewise, you can't expect learning to happen without first investing in it.

That means making a firm commitment to invest a certain amount of time and money in your own personal growth. Too many salespeople use a happenstance approach to learning. Rather than give it quality time and devote a portion of their regular workweek to it, they engage in it only in times left over from other duties. Learning becomes a hit-or-miss proposition.

If you were dedicated to becoming good at golf, you'd devote regular time to it, wouldn't you? You wouldn't allocate ten minutes at lunch and twenty minutes at night in front of the TV. You'd be much more serious about it, investing a significant amount of quality time. You might even begin every day with an hour or two on the golf course or at the driving range.

If you're going to gain mastery of learning as a competency, you must invest a sufficient amount of quality time. You've also got to spend some money and invest in yourself. If you wanted to become good at golf, you'd invest in lessons, in greens fees, in new clubs and shoes, and so on. In your attempt to become good at golf you would invest thousands of dollars. You'd be willing to pay that sum if you believed the payback would provide you an excellent return on that investment.

My company offers a service we call the Growth Coach. It's a one-on-one or small group coaching service, designed to help executives and salespeople grow their businesses and themselves more rapidly. Early in the process we ask our participants to decide how much time and money, on a monthly basis, they are willing to invest in their own learning. Then we ask them to make a written commitment.

I'm often asked, "How much time and money should I be investing?" Obviously, the ultimate answer is up to you. However, we've been able to develop some basic guidelines. We generally suggest investing a minimum of 5 percent of the workweek. If you're a typical salesperson, you work an average of forty-nine hours a week, so you'd invest two hours a week in learning. The 5 percent number seems to work well for the financial side of your investment also. If you take home an average of $4,000 a month, consider investing $200 of that in your own personal development.

Here's a simple, two-step process to help you implement these first two principles.

THE PROCESS

Step 1. Create a set of learning goals. Like so much of what we do, effective learning begins with a set of goals. Learning goals are different from performance goals. With a performance goal, you are

striving to sell certain things at certain levels. The focus is on the outside world—your territory, your customers, and your sales. A learning goal, however, is something that describes an improvement you want to make in yourself. It's internal rather than external, although the evidence of it could very well be obvious to other people.

For example, you might create a sales goal of exceeding your quota by 10 percent. That's a good goal, but it's a goal that describes how you perform in the outside world. You achieve this goal by influencing a sufficient quantity of other people to make decisions. On the other hand, you could create a learning goal that says, "I will become more adept at planning." That has nothing to do with other people; it has to do with you. The change will take place in you. That's a learning goal.

Your new-found skill in goal setting (see Chapter 11) can come into play here. Use that process to create a set of learning goals for yourself.

Step 2. Decide how much time and money you're going to invest. No goal is accomplished without effort, including learning goals. Reflect seriously, think carefully, and commit to a certain number of hours and dollars each week. Use the guidelines discussed earlier in this chapter.

⚓ *To become really effective at learning, you need to acquire good tools.*

Remember the golf example? If you were going to become really good at playing golf, you'd make sure you acquired the best tools (clubs, bags, balls, etc.). If you're going to become really good at learning, you'll need to acquire the best tools to do that.

You may be wondering what kinds of things could be learning tools. Web pages, encyclopedias, books, and newsletters all may come to mind. While these things could certainly be helpful, and we'll consider some of them in Chapter 14, they aren't the kind of tools I have in mind.

⏐ *From my perspective, the ultimate learning tool is* **a good question!**

That's right, a good question. Remember our discussion of questions in Chapter 7? The primary function of a good question is that it directs a person's thinking. In Chapter 7 we made use of this aspect of questions to create sales questions in order to direct our customers' thinking and help us understand our customers at deeper and more significant levels. Now we're going to use good questions to direct our own minds, to channel our own thinking, so that we can learn in a more effective manner.

The greatest teachers the world has known have used questions as primary tools to help their students learn. Think of the Socratic method. Socrates facilitated learning in his students by asking them questions. A whole method of teaching was developed, based on that tool.

The Bible is full of examples of Jesus Christ or God Himself interacting with people by asking them questions. Those questions were not asked in an attempt to gain information. They were asked to cause the questionee to think, and thereby to learn some powerful truth.

You've got the idea. A good question is like a key that unlocks the learning process. We can use good questions to unlock and open up the doors to information in three directions:

1. In the outside world,

2. In our own minds, and

3. In other people's minds.

Let's look at each direction.

QUESTIONS ABOUT THE OUTSIDE WORLD

When I use the term *outside world,* I'm referring to information that exists in the external environment, outside of your mind. Here's an example of this working in a routine, daily event.

My wife and I like to spend escape weekends in Detroit. (Really, you should try it some time.) We often stay with friends and, like most couples, it's not unusual for Coleen and her friend to go off shopping, while Paul and I watch a sporting event on TV.

On one of these occasions, Coleen came back and reported that they had found a great muffin bakery. Truly, this place was so good that it is almost worth the three-hour drive from our home in Grand Rapids.

Let's analyze how their discovery came to happen. I'm sure that they were driving down the road, or perhaps stopping at a strip mall, and noticed the muffin bakery. Probably, at that point, one of them said, or thought, something like, "I wonder what that bakery is like?" To satisfy their curiosity and answer that question, they stopped in, liked what they saw, sampled the muffins, and became enthusiastic converts. Now, every time we're in the northern suburbs of Detroit, we make it a point to stop in and buy some muffins.

We changed our behavior; we now always stop at the muffin store. We changed our behavior because of some new information we gathered—the great taste and variety of the muffins sold there. We gathered that information because someone thought or voiced a question. It was a question of the outside world, and it led us to new information, which led us to change our behavior. That's the definition of learning.

I recently read a story in a news magazine that discussed pharmaceutical company researchers who were searching through the plants of some of the world's rain forests in order to find new compounds that would become the basis for new drugs. Perhaps a cure for the common cold will be discovered. If and when that effective new compound is discovered it will be because someone asked the right question. The compound will have been there for eons. It will be older than the human race. But it would not have become effective unless one of those researchers asked the right question— "Is this compound effective against the common cold virus?" That question, asked of the outside world, could conceivably lead to new information; and that new information could lead to a change for all of us. The question is the key that unlocks truth and power in the world around us. Once we discover that, we learn.

When Albert Einstein discovered the law of relativity, the law itself was not new. It had been there, operating, since the creation of the universe. It took the person with the right question to discover it. Perhaps Einstein said to himself, "What is the relationship between E and MC^2?" When the right question was formulated, an incredible truth was learned. The question was the key.

When you ask questions about your accounts, your competition, or the products you sell, you're asking questions of the outside world. When you ask the planning questions mentioned in Chapter 4 regarding key account strategies, you're asking questions of the outside world.

I recently came across a great application of this principle. One of my clients, a distributor who represented dozens of manufacturers and had literally thousands of products to sell, had created a list of questions for salespeople to ask about any new product presented to them. When they asked those questions about the product, they gained new information. On the basis of that new information, they made decisions about which of the products to sell and how to sell them.

QUESTIONS TO UNLOCK INFORMATION IN OUR OWN MINDS

The older I become, the more convinced I am that we all carry around with us far more wisdom, knowledge, and insight than we ever use. Some pundits even claim that every perception we experience is stored in our minds as a memory. That would be every moment of every day, filed away in the files of our minds.

I have no way of knowing whether that is true. However, I am convinced that we are much wiser and more knowledgeable than we think we are. The missing link to unlocking the wisdom and knowledge we have is a good question. When we ask ourselves good questions, we unlock the knowledge and insights that are stored in our minds and bring them to a level at which we can implement them to make positive changes. For example, when you ask the question I suggested in Chapter 11—"Am I doing the most effective thing I could be doing right now?"—you're asking a question of yourself. You're forcing your mind to think about a certain thing.

When you take a few moments after a sales call and reflect on it, you're asking questions of yourself. Questions like, "What did I do well?" or "What could I have done differently?" or "What will be the most effective next step?" cause you to think about certain things and pull the information out of your head. You could, of course, just go onto the next sales call and never ask those questions of yourself. In that case, the information would have been stored in your mind, but never unleashed and used. It's the questions that cause the stored information to become useful to you.

QUESTIONS THAT UNLEASH INFORMATION IN OTHER PEOPLE'S MINDS

If you have a vast storehouse of information in your mind, imagine how much powerful, useful information is resident in the minds of all the people you encounter. Think about what you could learn if you could consistently tap into that vast treasury of powerful information.

When you ask questions of your customers, your manager, and your colleagues, you are unleashing the power of the information and insights stored in their heads. For example, when you ask your good customers the question, "What do you think we need to do in order to gain more business in this account?" you're tapping into the wisdom and insights in your customers' heads. When you ask your manager, "What can I do to improve my relationships with these two problem accounts?" you're tapping into the wisdom and insights in your manager's head. When you ask your colleagues, "What did you do this week that worked very well for you?" you're learning from the experiences and insights in their heads.

The world is full of powerful, useful information. You unleash that information by asking good questions. The question is the key. But you can waste time by asking useless questions. For example, you could have just walked out of a miserable sales call and thought to yourself, "Why does fate always go against me?" That question is probably not going to be worth the time it takes to think about it. It's a useless question.

Let's set up some standards to be guided by as we develop our questions.

⚓ *A good question uncovers pertinent information or useful insights, or moves the questioner closer to a positive future action.*

Let's look at each aspect of this principle. *Pertinent information* means information that is useful and salient to one of your learning goals. Look at the end result of the question—the information that will come in the form of an answer—and determine whether that information will be useful.

For example, the question "Why does fates always go against me?" doesn't uncover any useful information. However, if you were to rephrase the question to something like, "What am I doing that brings about a miserable sales call?" that question would bring you information that would ultimately be more usable. The question about fate will not result in information that will be useful. Regardless of what answer you come up with, you won't be able to do anything about it. However, the second question may uncover information that will eventually lead you to change your behavior. You don't have the time or energy to waste on useless questions.

A new *insight* is a conclusion you draw about something you already know. For example, you may know a certain product very well. You're familiar with all its features and applications. But suppose one day your manager asks you, "What is the single most attractive aspect of that product to your larger customers?" You've never thought about that. So you think about that question for a moment and reply, "They really like its simplicity. It's easy to use." That's an insight. You realize something that you never realized before. You always had the evidence for it, but you never consciously realized it before. Sometimes, good questions help you discover new insights about old information.

Finally, a good question moves you closer to a future, positive action. Remember, our definition of learning is dependent on behavior. If you don't change your behavior and act differently, you have not learned. Learning questions must move you to the point where you've identified a positive action you can take in the future. For example, it's one thing to ask yourself, "Why do I always make my customers irritated with me?" The answer would probably be good information to have. However, it won't be useful information unless you follow it up with another question: "What should I do differently in the future to make sure that doesn't happen again?" When you ask that question, you're moving closer to future, positive action.

As always, in order to unleash the power of this principle, you need a process. The process is what Chapter 14 is all about.

14

MASTER LEARNER: PART II

The Menta-Morphosis Process

The Sixth Hat is of such importance that I've given a unique name to the primary process involved. Menta-Morphosis is my name for a specific, powerful, self-directed learning process. It's name captures the sense of the principle on which it is based:

⚓ *You can change yourself and develop more rapidly by applying your mind to the task and changing your thinking.*

There is certainly nothing new about this principle. King Solomon, writing thousands of years ago in the book of Proverbs in the Bible, observed, "As a man thinks, so is he." The apostle Paul counseled the early Christians to "Be transformed by the renewing of your mind."

As always, what hinders us from applying this principle is lack of a how-to process. Menta-Morphosis is that process. It should be no surprise to you that the process is a series of steps, each characterized by a set of questions. Figure 14-1 graphically depicts the process.

Notice that this process is unique in that it is illustrated as a circle. It must be used over and over again. It's not a one-time task or activity, but rather a continuous way of life. Some of my clients have nicknamed this concept "Kahle's wheel."

Like all the other processes, this one consists of a number of steps, accomplished one at a time in the sequence in which they are presented. If you follow each step precisely and in the correct progression, you'll improve your performance—it's guaranteed!

Let's look at each step in the process.

FIGURE 14-1

The Menta-Morphosis Process for
Continuous Self-Directed Development

Step 1. Deepen the discontent. Learning, or changing your behavior, is not easy. In fact, for adults, it is one of the most difficult challenges we face. So many things work against it. For example, we have all built habits over the years. Changing one of those habits is difficult. I remember the first time I drove a rental car in South Africa, where they drive on the left instead of the right side of the street. After concentrating mightily, thinking through the moves I needed to make, and visualizing the car in traffic, I turned out of the parking lot directly into oncoming traffic! The habit of driving on the right side of the road was, at that point, stronger than I had anticipated it to be.

Of course, we all experience natural inertia. It's always easier to do what we are accustomed to doing. Maintaining the status quo is always the low-energy decision. It's been my observation, for example, that whenever salespeople have multiple responsibilities, and have operational tasks as well as proactive selling to do, the operational tasks expand to shrink the amount of time spent on proactive selling. It's a predictable phenomenon. Why is that? Because it's easier to deal with things that come our way, to react, then it is to be proactive. Our natural inertia keeps us sitting at our desk, rationalizing the things we're doing, rather than being out in the car creating new relationships with customers.

Understanding this, we need to do whatever we can do to improve our chances of actually making positive changes. That means that we need to load as much power into our change process as we can.

The power, energy, and motivation to change come from discontent. The people most likely to change are those who are most discontent with the status quo, and the opposite is also true. Those least likely to change are those who are most content with the current situation. Reflect a bit on this, and you'll realize that it is true. One of the most common complaints I hear in my work as a sales consultant is the complaint from sales managers that they can't motivate some of their senior salespeople. The reason? The senior salespeople are content. They're making enough money, they've achieved many of their goals, and they therefore see no reason to change.

The same is true for you. If you're perfectly content, you're not going to change or grow. If you're discontent, then you'll have the power to expend the energy it takes to make changes. Therefore, if you're going to become good at the sixth hat, Master Learner, you need to learn how to create discontent in yourself. You need to make that discontent as deep and powerful as you can.

How do you create a situation of deep discontent?

START BY RECOGNIZING YOUR NEED TO IMPROVE

You need to grow and improve. When you make this realization, you've entered the process. The realization can come from either of two sources—pain or gain. You either want to eliminate a situation that troubles you (pain) or you want to gain something you don't now have. Without this internal motivation, you won't be sufficiently energized to stretch yourself out of your comfort zones and develop new habits.

For example, you might be sick of your manager complaining about your lack of new customers. You want to do away with that pain. You're discontent with the way things are and you want to eliminate that negative, nagging pressure.

On the other hand, you might want to add something positive to your life. You'd really like to have a new BMW. Not that your Taurus is a problem; you'd just like to have something that you don't have now. So your discontent is channeled to a positive thing—gaining something you don't have now.

A little thought at this point will soon make clear the significant role of goal setting in providing motivation to change and improve. When you set a goal, you create healthy discontent. In other words, you create a situation in which you want something positive that you don't now have. To make this step work for you, identify some pain or gain in your life, and turn that into a goal.

It doesn't matter whether the source is positive or negative. The important thing is that you have transformed it, through the goal-setting process described in Chapter 11, into a motivating goal. You've created some discontent. That discontent is the beginning of motivation. Motivation is the power that stimulates and energizes the system.

The beginning point in the process is your realization that you want to eliminate some pain or realize some gain in your life. I should point out that, while this system discusses sales improvement and it appears in a sales book, it can be applied to any area of your life. It doesn't matter whether you want to improve your prospecting skills or your parenting skills, acquire new customers or lose extra weight—the system can be used for any area of personal improvement.

One way to attack step one is to create learning goals for yourself. But there is another, deeper way.

CRYSTALIZING YOUR PERSONAL MISSION

Here's an alternate way of creating discontent. Of the two, this is the method I prefer. Before we focus on this technique, we need to discuss a concept depicted in Figure 14-2. You'll recognize the graphic from Chapter 11. It's our onion analogy again, only this time the onion is you. The layers of onion represent levels of depth in you.

On the very surface are your interactions with other people— your customers and prospects. These interactions are often shaped and directed by the sales tactics we've been talking about. This is the *you* that your customers see. For example, you might ask a customer a series of good questions, wearing the Effective Consultant hat. That series of questions is a tactic—the very surface of who you are. If over a period of time, you develop that practice of asking questions effectively, you've created a skill. Good for you; that's important. However, in the larger picture of everything that you are, it's the most superficial part of you.

As we peel each layer off the onion, we go deeper into the person you are. Just beneath the surface are the strategies you design, the goals you set, the habits you have built up over the years, and the ways you go about doing things. For example, let's say you ask

FIGURE 14-2

Personal Growth from the Inside Out

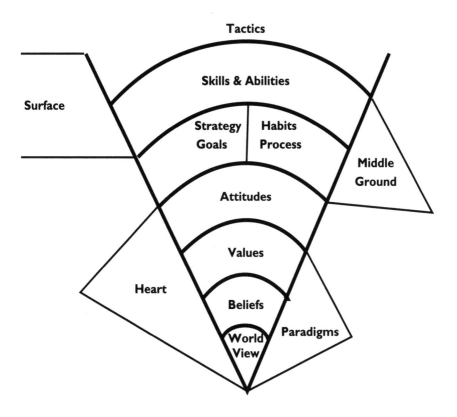

your customer good questions. That's a tactic, on the very surface of your being. It's where you interact with someone else. The reason you ask questions—the motivating force that underlies your use of that tactic—can be any one of four things.

Perhaps it arises out of a strategic plan you created to learn more about your customer. The strategy was the deeper motivation that gave rise to the more superficial tactic. You might have developed a goal to ask four questions during the course of the day. In that case, the goal was the deeper motivation. Maybe it's just your habit to always ask good questions. You're not really sure why you developed that habit. In that case, the habit was the deeper issue that caused you to ask those questions. Finally, the deeper issue could be a process you've created that requires you to fill out a form with the answer to that question.

Your sales behavior always arises out of one of those four motivations. You either work intentionally, with planning and forethought, as evidenced by your goals, strategies, and processes, or you work unconsciously, through your habits and routines. These motivating forces lie just beneath the surface, but they shape your actual behavior.

Peel off the outer layer of the onion and you'll find, at the next deepest level, your attitudes. You've heard many times about the importance of a good attitude. That's because your attitudes give rise to your habits and your goals.

When you're burdened with a depressed, pessimistic attitude, you don't set worthwhile goals or aspire to great accomplishments. The opposite is also true. When you have a positive, optimistic attitude, you naturally aspire to challenging goals, and that leads to energy and positive behavior. If your attitude is positive, you'll feel that you can positively influence a prospect. That positive attitude can lead you to creating a goal and developing the strategy that you'll need to achieve the goal.

Going back to the example of asking questions, let's suppose your positive attitude has led you to develop the goal of acquiring three new accounts this month. Now that you are optimistic enough to set a challenging goal, you need to create a strategy to achieve it. You decide on a strategy, part of which requires you to ask good questions of a certain number of prospects. In this example, your attitude led to a goal, which led to a strategy, which led to the actions you took with your prospect. Your actions bubbled up from the inside out.

But you're still not at the very heart of things. Underlying your attitudes are your values. Values are the things you hold dear and important. For example, you might value integrity, success in your job, and the well-being of your spouse very highly. These values give rise to certain attitudes about those things.

Take the example of highly valuing your spouse's physical well-being. Because you value him or her so highly, you think positively about your ability to provide protection and security. Out of that attitude arise your goals and strategies.

But you're still not finished. Underlying and supporting your values are your beliefs. For example, you may believe that it is always the husband's responsibility to support the family, no matter what. This belief may be so deep inside you that you've never really articulated it. It's just been embedded deep in your psyche. As a result of that belief, you place a high value on the physical well-being of your spouse because, after all, it's your job to take care of that. That value leads to attitudes, which lead to goals or habits, which lead to behavior.

There is yet one deeper layer, the heart of the onion, and that is your worldview. Your worldview is comprised of your fundamental, core beliefs about the world and yourself. It's composed of the absolute deepest beliefs you hold about your purpose in life and the way in which the world functions. It differs from the beliefs above it only in degree. The worldview comprises the beginning of the spiritual part of ourselves. These beliefs shape everything above them.

For example, one person may believe that the universe is so connected that everything we do is a result of fate or destiny. Another individual may believe the opposite, that we are creatures with free will existing in a world that responds to us. A third may believe that we are the creations of a loving God, designed for a specific purpose.

If you hold a worldview that attributes everything that happens to you to fate or destiny, you'll have little interest in building positive attitudes, creating goals, developing strategies, practicing skills, and using effective tactics. I've personally seen tribal people in developing countries who hold such worldviews. As a group, they never seem to make much progress, and many of their lifestyles and economic conditions have changed little over the generations. The lack of improvement in their conditions is, in my opinion, a function of their worldview. In many cases, millions of dollars of aid and years of assistance at the more superficial levels have done little. Real change won't take place until they make changes in their worldview.

This basic view of yourself and the world is usually influenced by your culture. It is often influenced by religious education, because it borders on the spiritual part of us.

Now, you're probably wondering what all this has to do with sales. Study the illustration. Notice that there is a direct relationship between the higher layers and the deeper layers. When changes are made in the deeper layers, those changes affect everything above them. Because of the structure of the onion, a small change made deep down in a person will affect almost everything above it. If you change your attitudes, you'll change your strategy, habits, and actions. Change your values and your beliefs, and you can't help but change your attitudes. Modify your worldview, and everything above it will change.

Now, suppose you were to crystallize one part of your world-view—the image you have of yourself. Suppose you were to see yourself as a unique entity with a unique place and purpose. Suppose you were to think about this unique purpose and project forward to the point that you had become almost everything you were capable of becoming, doing exactly the work you were meant to do, using the unique combination of competencies and life experiences you have accumulated along the way. Finally, suppose you were able to crystallize and articulate that vision of yourself. Would that vision of who you could become provide sufficient discontent with your current situation to power your self-directed development?

Of course it would, and that brings us to the second way to deepen the discontent. Uncover and articulate your vision of who you are meant to become; resolve the question of your purpose in life. Keeping that vision in front of you provides the power of discontent simply because you are not now who or what you want to be. The gap between who you were meant to become and who you are now represents the discontent that powers your efforts.

I once taught an intense, ten-week sales training program in which the first week was given to a discussion of worldviews and the first assignment was to write a statement of your purpose in life. Why bother? Because the more completely you resolve the deeper issues, the more likely it is that you will have congruence, not conflict, in all the layers above. I have never met a consistently successful professional salesperson who hadn't calmly and confidently resolved the deeper issues. I have met hundreds of salespeople who have had short-term success, sometimes spectacular success, but whose lack of deeper grounding spun them out of control, crashing and burning in some self-defeating behavior.

To add power to the process of making significant, long-lasting, permanent changes in your results, resolve the deeper issues in your life. When you're finished with this step, you've answered the question, "Why should I learn?" You've loaded some power into the learning process.

Step 2. Generate good ideas. Now it's time to generate some ideas. You have your goals, but you haven't developed ways to reach them. That's where "good ideas" come in. A good idea is a possibility, some way you can achieve all or part of your goals.

This step in the Menta-Morphosis process involves generating and collecting multitudes of good ideas. Good ideas are all around you. You only need to learn how to recognize and capture them.

Generating ideas is an essential step. Think about it: If your goal is to change yourself in some way, you must act differently. Before you can act differently, you must decide how to act. Before you can decide how to act, you must have some idea of the possible actions you can take that will bring you positive results. So you must develop some ideas before you can act differently. Figure 14-3 illustrates how this works.

FIGURE 14-3

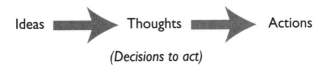

(Decisions to act)

The process starts with good ideas. Generating good ideas—ideas about how you can make changes and act differently in order to reach your goals—is a necessary step.

You can generate good ideas in two basic ways:

1. Inject yourself into learning opportunities.
2. Reflect on past experiences.

Let's explore each way.

INJECT YOURSELF INTO LEARNING OPPORTUNITIES

A learning opportunity is an experience whereby you come into contact with new information or you develop new insights.

Learning opportunities can take many forms. Here's a list of some of the most common learning opportunities:

- Seminars and workshops
- Classes sponsored by educational institutions
- Small-group discussions with your peers
- Company meetings
- Coaching sessions
- Conversations with your bosses or managers
- Books
- Audio and video tapes
- Articles in periodicals
- Articles and Web pages on the Internet
- Educational television programs
- Conversations with friends and associates
- Telephone conferences
- Video conferences
- Watching a role model
- Talking with a mentor

For the rest of your working life, you'll need to regularly inject yourself into some of these learning opportunities. Your company may provide you with some opportunities, but you shouldn't rely solely on the company to provide learning opportunities for you. If you're going to be in charge of your own learning, you must take the initiative yourself. Remember the earlier principle: *Learning is your primary responsibility.*

TURNING GOALS INTO QUESTIONS

One of the best ways to begin is to turn your learning goals into questions. For example, one of your learning goals might be, "To get along better with my branch manager." If you started to work at that goal, you'd naturally develop some questions, such as:

- *What can I do differently to get along with my branch manager?*
- *What is the best way for me to get along with my branch manager?*

Each of these questions focuses on things you control, is pointed toward the future, and directly relates to the goal.

The process of turning a goal into a major question or two will help you to select appropriate learning opportunities. For example, if you decide that you want to improve your relationship with your branch manager, you might begin by looking for a seminar on interpersonal skills. You might look for an opportunity to talk with your peers about how they do it, or maybe even have a conversation with a mentor about it.

When you've identified and entered into a learning opportunity, it's time to use that opportunity to generate ideas.

GENERATING GOOD IDEAS FROM LEARNING OPPORTUNITIES

Let's assume that you're reading a book as one of your learning opportunities. Remember, the purpose of reading the book is simple: to generate good ideas or to stimulate new insights. It's nice that the book looks good on your bookshelf, impresses your friends, and gives you something to talk about in social conversations, but all of that is extraneous. It's nice, but not important.

If you chose the book well, it should provide you with some information or insights that you didn't have before. That's good, but it's only a means to an end. New information is helpful as long as it leads to good ideas. Remember the definition of a good idea. It's an idea that focuses on the future and describes potential behavior—things you can *do* differently. If the information you've acquired doesn't lead to good ideas, it's not worth the time it takes to ingest that information. Information or insights that don't lead to good ideas are impotent. The only useful purpose for the time you spend reading the book, or being involved in any learning opportunity, is the generation of good ideas.

The question is, "How do you generate good ideas?"

The answer is to ask yourself questions. As you ask yourself questions, you prompt your mind to reflect on the ideas and content of the book. That thought process leads to good ideas. It really is that simple.

Here are two sets of questions to ask. Establish the discipline of asking yourself these questions after you read any section of a book, attend a seminar, listen to a tape, or engage in any learning opportunity.

- *In this section, were there any insights to be gained?* (Remember the definition of an insight from Chapter 13.)

- *How does that insight apply to my situation?*

- *What could I do differently?*

This series of questions asks you to first identify insights, and then generate ideas from those insights. The diagram of the process looks like Figure 14-4.

FIGURE 14-4

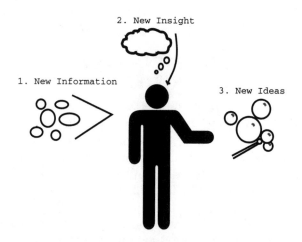

As an alternative, try skipping the first two questions and leaping right to the heart of the matter with this question:

- *Did this section give me any ideas about ways in which I can do things differently?*

This is a simpler approach and works for some people, some of the time. The diagram of this approach looks like Figure 14-5.

FIGURE 14-5

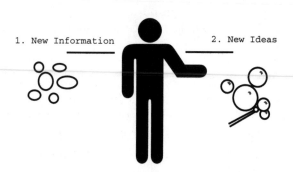

Here's one more variation on the technique. Ask yourself the questions *before* you read the chapter, attend the seminar, or listen to the tape. This technique programs your subconscious mind and directs it to look for the answers to the questions. When you ask yourself the questions in advance, you will find yourself coming up with answers as you read or listen. Just make sure that you allow yourself time at the end of each section to reflect on that section a bit, and wait for the answers to appear.

The process of asking yourself questions is the basic technology for generating ideas regardless of the type of learning opportunity. You ask the same questions whether you are reading a book, attending a seminar, joining in a discussion group, or taking part in a teleconference.

Let's go back to our example of reading a book. As you read, you stop momentarily after each section and ask yourself the questions listed. For example, you may be reading a book on interpersonal skills, and the book talks about adjusting to different personality styles. You realize that your branch manager has one kind of personality style, and you have another. Good! You've acquired an *insight*. Now you think some more about it, asking yourself the question, "How does that insight apply to my situation?" You think, "That might be part of the problem. I want him to be like me, and it irritates me that he doesn't act or think the way I do."

Now ask yourself the last question, "What could I do differently?" You answer yourself, "I should try to appreciate his style as a complement to mine." Good! That's a good idea.

Now, before you go any further, capture that good idea. Write it down. Imagine a bubble wand and a bottle of bubble liquid. We've all waved these wands through the air and produced dozens of bubbles. With the right combination of materials and motion, you can use the bubble wand to fill the air with bubbles. Good ideas are like those bubbles. The right combination of materials (your experiences) and motions (your thought processes) will result in dozens of good ideas.

After you've captured the good idea, continue on with the book or the learning experience in which you're involved. As you do that, you'll develop a whole file of good ideas. You'll work with them later. Right now, the important thing is that you use your learning opportunities to generate good ideas. Whenever you generate one, stop and write it down.

REFLECT ON PAST EXPERIENCES: THE SERENDIPITY APPROACH

So far, we've been discussing a *targeted approach* to generating good ideas. In other words, you've decided beforehand what you wanted to learn, planned for appropriate learning opportunities, and created ideas from those experiences. That proactive approach is necessary and effective.

But not all learning takes place in that way. Sometimes we learn in a less targeted way, in a way I call the *serendipity approach*. The dictionary defines *serendipity* as the "process of making happy, chance discoveries." We can make happy, chance learning discoveries.

Here's how it works. Let's say you just had a very good conversation with your branch manager. You enjoyed it and felt good about it. You and he finally seemed to communicate. After the experience, as you're driving home, you mentally review the conversation. Often, that's as far as we take it. But suppose you were to reflect on the experience you just had and ask yourself the question, "What was it that made this such a good experience?" As you think about that question, you come up with these answers:

- We both found something we thought was funny, and laughed about it together.
- I didn't feel the usual tension I feel with him.
- I wasn't looking for something to find fault with.

Now there's one more question for you to reflect on: "Does that experience prompt any ideas about how you should act in the future?"

As you think about that question, you come up with these ideas:

- I should find something we can laugh about together.
- I should not look for things to find fault with or object to.

Do you know what you just did? You generated some good ideas. Only this time, the good ideas came from an experience that you had, one from which you didn't necessarily intend to learn. It was a happy, chance discovery.

The primary thinking technology used in serendipity learning is the process of reflecting. Reflecting is simply the process of thinking about your experiences and generating ideas from those experiences. You engage in the process of reflection simply by asking yourself questions and developing the answers. You can use this simple process whenever you have an experience that seems particularly successful or unsuccessful. Reflect on it by asking yourself these questions:

- *What was it that made this so [successful, unsuccessful]?*
- *What can I learn from that?*
- *What ideas does this give me for the future?*
- *What could I do differently in the future?*

Not only can you reflect on a specific incident or experience, you can also reflect on a much wider set of experiences. Let's go back to the same goal, "To achieve a great relationship with my branch manager." You can choose to reflect on your life! Set aside some time and focus your thinking. Here are some questions you could ask yourself in order to help generate some good ideas.

> *"Have I ever been in a similar situation, where I didn't get along with someone in authority?"*

> *"Have I ever been in a situation where I was the manager or person in authority, and didn't get along with someone?"*

> *"What happened in each of those situations? Did the relationship get better or worse? What did the person being managed do to improve or detract from the relationship?"*

> *"If that were true of that situation, would it be true of this situation?"*

> *"What can I do, based on what I've already experienced, that might work in the current situation?"*

When you ask yourself the last question, you may well generate some ideas that you can use to achieve your goal. That's how reflection works. You might want to schedule some time for reflection on each of your goals.

Now you have two means of generating good ideas: 1) injecting yourself into learning opportunities, and 2) serendipity, or reflecting on past experiences. The end result of both is a list of good ideas.

Once you're comfortable generating good ideas, it's time to move to the next step—using the ideas to help you reach your goals.

One last thought: It's amazing how our minds work. Once you give it the job of creating good ideas, your subconscious mind will accept that task and begin to work on it. When it has done some subconscious reflection, it may well spit out the good ideas it created. You may, therefore, be driving in your car, watching TV, reading a good book, or barbecuing for the family when a good idea strikes you. Don't let it go. Write it down immediately. If you don't write it down immediately, you will probably lose it and never capture it again.

Your job now is to distill several good ideas out of that information, which brings us to the next step in the process.

Step 3. Distill the best. The easy part is over. If you go no further than this point—and that's what most people do—you've just wasted your time. You're like the person who makes New Year's resolutions but never follows through on them. You're satisfied with good ideas and vague intentions. If you want to get serious, you must progress through the rest of the process.

This step requires you to select some of the good ideas that you wish to implement. Sort through the ideas and identify the best of them. I call this distilling the best. The process of distilling the best, like all the other thinking and learning processes, is a matter of asking yourself questions and developing the answers. Sift through your ideas by asking yourself these questions:

- *Which one or two of these ideas could have the **fastest** impact on achieving your goals?*

- *Which one or two of these ideas could have the **biggest** impact on achieving your goals?*

- *Which one or two of these ideas would be the **easiest** for you to implement?*

- *Which one or two ideas are you **most passionate** about?*

I suggest that you look over the list of ideas and pick no more than three. For example, suppose you read a book on sales—this one! As a result, you created a list of good ideas. Your list looks like this:

- Get better organized.
- Create account and personal profiles.
- Ask better questions.

- Focus on knowing my customers more deeply and broadly.
- Develop creative proposals.
- Implement "learned optimism."
- Create annual and quarterly personal goals.
- Create monthly strategic plans for my A accounts.
- Work at continuous improvement.

Now, even I'll admit that this is an ambitious agenda. Realistically, you're not going to be able to implement all of these ideas right away. Prioritize by selecting the three good ideas that you think will have the greatest potential effect on your performance. Let's consider the following examples:

- Get better organized.
- Ask better questions.
- Create monthly strategic plans for my A accounts.

What about the rest of the ideas you generated? Are they worthless? Not at all; they're just not the highest priority at this moment. Create another file for yourself. Label this one, "Good ideas," and put your list and all the supporting notes for those ideas into that file. When you've completed "Kahle's wheel," and you have successfully implemented your current high-priority list, the others will be there for you to consider again.

When you have arrived at this point, you've successfully completed step three. As you may have surmised, the step of distilling the best is a process that needs to be repeated on a regular basis. You can do it after every major learning experience or on a preset schedule. Try to set aside some time at least once a month to devote to the process of distilling the best of your ideas.

Step 4. Precisely prescribe. This is the step that separates the serious learners from those who only toy with the process. This is hard work. This step requires you to move from good ideas and vague intentions to specific commitments for changing your behavior in precise ways.

To bridge that gap, you must translate each of your good ideas into precise prescriptions by rewriting each idea, beginning with the words, "I will...."

As an example, let's work on the good idea, "Avoid finding fault with my branch manager." Rewrite it to read, "I will avoid finding fault with my branch manager." Sounds good, but it's a little too vague to really help you change. You need to rewrite it to make it more specific. "I will avoid finding fault with my branch manager every day. I will dismiss negative thoughts as soon as they come into my head, and I will never voice them to anyone."

That's much better because it's more specific. It's achievable and realistic. But you're not home yet. Make sure that your statement meets two criteria:

1. It expresses behavior that someone else can witness.
2. At the end of the day, you can ask yourself whether or not you did what you said you were going to do, and you can answer that question with a simple "yes" or "no."

Let's go back to the example. You have written the statement, "I will …." Does that express behavior that someone else can witness? Can a tiny, invisible manager who rides around on your shoulder all day witness you doing that? She couldn't see your thoughts, but she could observe your words so, this statement counts. Your statement meets the first criterion.

Now consider your statement in light of the second criterion. Is it something that, at the end of the day, you can ask yourself, "Did I do this?" and answer yes or no? At the end of the day, can you say "Yes, I did it, or "No, I didn't?" Yes, you can. Your statement meets the second criterion.

Like the previous process, the step of precisely prescribing should be repeated regularly. Try to do it at least once a month, as well as after a particularly effective learning experience.

When you have completed this step, you will have succeeded at the crucial step of translating your good ideas and vague intentions into precise prescriptions for your future behavior. You've completed one of the most difficult tasks in my system. You're now ready for the next step.

Step 5. Act. This is the hardest part of the whole system. It's just so easy to keep on doing the things that we've always done. We're

comfortable with them. But if you're going to make any progress, if you're serious about learning and growing, then you must act. You must stretch yourself and do something that you might never have done before. You'll push yourself outside of your comfort zone to the risky area of behaving in some new way.

This is almost always difficult and laden with fear and anxiety. You'll make the task easier by following the Menta-Morphosis process to this point. Doing so establishes the logical reasons to change and try something new. It also defines your new behavior very precisely and thus makes it easier to do. You've stacked the deck on your side to make it easier for you to improve.

All you have to do now is do it. Easier said than done. A helpful technique that will help you translate your ideas into action is to publish your prescriptions. That means that you share your intentions with someone else. The fact that you've made your prescriptions public, that other people know about them, adds pressure on you to actually do what you say you're going to do.

Then just do it. The first time is the most difficult. Once you've done the thing once, you'll find it much easier to do it again, and then again, and so on until you've repeated the new behavior enough to make it a habit.

Here's a technique that will help you focus on turning your new behaviors into actions. Figure 14-6 is a form on which to keep track of your progress. Use it like this:

FIGURE 14-6

Sales Habit Builder

Month _____

Activity	1	2	3	4	5	6	7	8	9	10	11	12	13	14	15	16	17	18	19	20	21	22	23	24	25	26	27	28	29	30	31

Turn each of your precise prescriptions into one- or two-word descriptions. For example, your prescription about getting along with your branch manager reads, "I will avoid finding fault with my branch manager every day. I will dismiss negative thoughts as soon as they come into my head, and I will never voice them to anyone." Turn that into the two-word description, "No negatives." Write that description in the wide column on the left of the form.

At the end of each day, ask yourself the question, "Did I do today what I said I was going to do?" In other words, did you eliminate all negative thoughts about your branch manager today? If you can honestly answer "Yes," then mark an X in the space for today's date. If the answer is "No," put a zero in the space.

Some behaviors you can work on daily. They're what the 1 to 31 blocks are for. Others are behaviors you repeat weekly. Use the wider blocks (five spaces per month) to record your progress on those.

Repeat this short step every day. The thirty seconds or so that it takes each day to do this will keep your prescriptions firmly planted in your mind, and keep you focused on making the changes you said you were going to make.

When you have acted by doing the things that you said you were going to do a number of times, then it's time to move on to the next step.

Step 6: Fine-tune. Generally, you don't get it right the first few times you try something new. That means that you must refine what you're doing, making fine-tuning changes in your actions in order to bring about the results you want. In fact, you might have to repeat this process several times, continually trying, then making small revisions and trying again, until you finally achieve that kind of behavior you're looking for. Think of golf as an example. How many fine-tuning adjustments does it take to come up with the perfect swing?

The process for fine-tuning is similar to the reflection process for generating ideas. After you've had the experience of trying some new behavior, you reflect on your experience by asking yourself questions. Use these questions:

- *Did I do what I said I was going to do?*
- *Why or why not?*

- *What happened as a result of my actions?*
- *What can I learn from this?*
- *What should I do differently the next time?*

As you ask yourself these questions, you focus your mind on your behavior and the results of your actions. You develop answers, and those answers can serve as ideas and insights. As you review the answers to your questions, decide what you're going to do differently the next time by distilling the best of the ideas you come up with, and then precisely prescribing your action.

You're making fine-tuning changes, small adjustments that move you closer to the competency for which you're striving. Continue this process of acting and refining until you've arrived at a degree of competency that you're happy with. At that point, you can honestly say that you've learned. You've changed your behavior in a positive way. You're a different, more capable, more competent person.

Perhaps more importantly, you've learned a process you can use to accelerate your learning for the rest of your life. You can now use the process and principles of the sixth hat to implement the principles of the other hats. But that's only one of dozens of applications. You can use the same process to grow and develop in every area of your life. Whether you want to be a better manager, salesperson, friend, or spouse, a more effective parent, or a more sensitive spirit, you can use Menta-Morphosis to fuel your growth. That's the power of the Menta-Morphosis process. Once you learn the system, you can use it over and over again. The Menta-Morphosis process will serve you well forever.

Now it's up to you to continue.

Trying on the Sixth Hat

The amount of material contained in this hat isn't as great as in some of the other hats. However, the impact this set of competencies can have on your career and your sales performance is immeasurable. Let's review.

We discussed these principles:

1. *Learning is the process of taking in new information or developing new insights, and then changing your behavior in positive ways as a result.*

2. *Learning is your primary responsibility.*

3. *In order to become good at learning, you must invest in it.*

4. *To become really effective at learning, you need to acquire good tools.*

5. *A good question uncovers pertinent information or useful insights, or moves the questioner closer to a positive future action.*

6. *You can change yourself and develop more rapidly by applying your mind to the task and changing your thinking.*

One master process incorporates all of these principles: the Menta-Morphosis process. Becoming a master of continuous, systematic, self-directed learning requires that you learn and use that process. It will enable you to change effectively and efficiently. Master it, and you'll be able to use it over and over for the rest of your life. It will help accelerate your career growth as it helps you to grow and add new competencies.

Unfortunately, there is no shortcut. The way to begin trying on this hat is to dig in at step one, *deepening the discontent.* Set aside some time in the next week or so to develop your career and learning goals, to commit some resources to them, and to think deeply about the rewards and consequences of achieving them. You should repeat this step at least once a year.

When you've created goals and made some commitments for resources, move on to the next step, *generating ideas.* As soon as you can, make a commitment to some learning opportunity. It may be a seminar or a tape or another book. Review the list of typical learning opportunities, and get involved in *something.*

Then, as you experience the learning opportunity, focus on collecting usable ideas. Create a big list. You might even want to categorize them and file them away in an electronic or manila folder. I use a special Post-it note to write down my good ideas, and then file them in one of about eight different categories.

The third step is to *distill the best* of those ideas, a process of categorizing, editing, and prioritizing. After you have some ideas in your list, review them and select the two or three that you want to focus on initially.

Step four requires you to translate those selected ideas into *precise prescriptions* for your behavior. Review this chapter to see how to do that.

Step five requires you to *act* in those new and positive ways, a never-ending daily challenge.

Step six involves *fine-tuning* and repeating the new behaviors until you reach a level of competency. The process of reviewing your actions and their consequences is really a repetition of steps 2, 3, 4, and 5. It should be a formal, monthly discipline, but you can engage in it more frequently.

That brings you back to where you started. Now begin the whole process over again.

Wearing the Sixth Hat

If anything characterizes masters of the sixth hat, it is rapid, continuous personal development. When you're continually implementing this hat, you'll be moving forward in your career more rapidly, seeing more success in your sales performance, and even living a more fulfilling life. Remember, the Menta-Morphosis process is not just for sales. Use it to grow in every area of your life.

When you've fully implemented the competencies of this hat, you'll be devoting a generous amount of time and resources to your own personal development. The Menta-Morphosis process will become a regular part of your routine.

Here's a list of the steps and their recommended frequency:

1. Deepening the discontent   —   Annually
2. Generating ideas   —   Daily
3. Distilling the best   —   Monthly
4. Precisely prescribing   —   Monthly
5. Acting   —   Daily
6. Refining   —   Monthly

As you repeat the process, you will find yourself becoming a master of systematic, self-directed learning, wearing the sixth hat. That is the ultimate success skill for the Information Age.

APPLICATION: USING THE SIX HATS TO TURN CHALLENGES INTO OPPORTUNITIES

Challenge: Just when I get comfortable with some method or product, my company changes it. It seems that I'm in a constant state of confusion. I could do a much better job of selling if I had some stability in my company.

I can empathize. Countless numbers of salespeople have confided very similar thoughts to me at seminars and training programs. Compensation plans change, territories evolve, inside staff turns over, new programs and products come and go—it's hard to keep focused when the internal support you count on seems as sure and solid as a bowl of Jell-O.

Unfortunately, this is probably not a temporary phenomenon. Let's go all the way back to where we began, with an understanding that the world around us is changing at an ever-increasing rate. In all likelihood, your company is doing so also. Even if they aren't today, they will probably be doing so tomorrow.

It's not going to go away. This constant change, both inside your organization and outside, is the hallmark of the Information Age. You don't have many options for dealing with this change.

You can drop out—refuse to change, refuse to adjust, and give up. Maybe you would be happier living on welfare.

"Okay," you're thinking, "that's really drastic. Certainly there are other options."

You can find employment that isn't so demanding, but the issue of rapid change won't go away. You can't escape it. Ask anyone in the jobs you might consider whether things are changing rapidly for them. Listen to them say the same things you are thinking. In any job you take, you're going to need to deal with rapid change. If you want to avoid dealing with rapid change, you've got to drop out of the economic system.

What other options do you have? You could live, for awhile, in denial. Nod your head at sales meetings, offer lip service to your manager, and go about doing your job the way you've always done it, pretending that you can get by without changing. How long will you last? In most organizations, that approach will catch up with you in a few months. So unless you make alternate employment arrangements within that period of time, denial isn't a viable strategy.

The last option is really the best option. It comes down to this: You've got to change. You've got to be able to be flexible, to adjust, to change the way you do your job, to change the tools you use, to change your approaches and your methods. If you're going to survive and prosper, you must become a master of personal change.

At my presentations and sales seminars, I am almost always asked a version of this question by a manager or business owner: "How do I get my salespeople to change?"

I often respond by relating a real-life experience of one of my clients. After studying the issue of sales force automation thoroughly, my client decided to automate his sales force of six outside salespeople. He developed his own contact management and sales forecasting software, and invested in laptop computers for each salesperson. His requirement of them was that they type in a two-minute sales call report after each sales call, answering several specific questions. Recognizing that some of them didn't know how to type, he offered to pay for typing classes for them, and required that they complete those classes in the next eight months.

Four of the salespeople quietly—not arrogantly, not boisterously, not confrontationally—decided not to do so. Their position was this: "We're professional salespeople. We make our living selling. We're not clerks. We don't need to type. Since when do salespeople need to know how to type?"

My client's position was this: "Since when do salespeople need to know how to type? Since now. This is how we're going to go to market. This is how we're going to make sales in this company. If you don't learn to type, you can't do sales the way we do it."

The net result was that the four salespeople were replaced. I wholeheartedly supported my client in that decision.

The need to change and grow and develop is the fundamental success skill in the Information Age. If people fight you on this issue, they will continue to defy you on others. Today it's the computer, tomorrow it's a new compensation plan, then it's a new product line, program, or approach to the market, a new territory or a new presentation. It doesn't matter what it is. The underlying skill, the operational attitude is the *ability and propensity to change*. In dealing with the issue of rapid internal change or rapid external change, the only really effective option is to learn to change yourself.

The Six Hats are your keys to continuous success in a rapidly changing world. The principles are the anchors you can count on to stabilize and support your sales efforts for the rest of your career. The processes provide the bridges from your understanding of the principles to effectively implementing them in your life. The combination of the two will empower you to successfully adjust to changing circumstances, no matter what they are.

Use the Six Hats wisely.

INDEX